THE CARPENTER'S SON

THE CARPENTER'S SON

*A Proletarian Reconstruction
of Jesus of Nazareth*

BY
Christian Chiakulas

WIPF & STOCK · Eugene, Oregon

THE CARPENTER'S SON
A Proletarian Reconstruction of Jesus of Nazareth

Copyright © 2019 Christian Chiakulas. All rights reserved. Except for brief quotations in critical publications or reviews, no part of this book may be reproduced in any manner without prior written permission from the publisher. Write: Permissions, Wipf and Stock Publishers, 199 W. 8th Ave., Suite 3, Eugene, OR 97401.

Wipf & Stock
An Imprint of Wipf and Stock Publishers
199 W. 8th Ave., Suite 3
Eugene, OR 97401

www.wipfandstock.com

PAPERBACK ISBN: 978-1-5326-9507-0
HARDCOVER ISBN: 978-1-5326-9508-7
EBOOK ISBN: 978-1-5326-9509-4

Manufactured in the U.S.A.   11/14/19

For Sara, whose love and support made this book possible

CONTENTS

Preface | ix
Acknowledgments | xi
Introduction | xiii

Chapter 1—FOUNDATION | 1
Chapter 2—HISTORICAL CONTEXT | 22
Chapter 3—PRACTICE | 44
Chapter 4—THEORY | 93
Chapter 5—PASSION | 132
Chapter 6—RESURRECTION | 148
Epilogue—THE GOOD NEWS | 166

Bibliography | 173
Subject Index | 175
Ancient Document Index | 177

PREFACE

I wrote the book you're about to read between working as a delivery driver, trying to finish a bachelor's degree online, and taking care of my four-year-old daughter. This is important to talk about up front because I consider this book to be semi-academic. I hope I've written it in language that anybody interested in this topic can understand, but I have also tried very hard to cite my sources and show the incredible amount of research that went into this book. With any work of nonfiction that purports to educate people, whether the subject be history, theology, or political theory (and this book is a bit of all three), the credentials of the author are likely to be scrutinized in direct proportion to the controversiality of the claims.

I expect that there is much in this book that people will find challenging. Whether it becomes popular enough to be controversial is another matter, but if that does happen, even on a small scale, I expect many of the ivory-tower-academic types to dismiss my arguments outright because when I wrote it I still had not obtained a degree and am not a professional scholar. To those people I can only shrug, and hope that those with fewer prejudices will at least engage with the argument in order to discredit it.

Western academia has always been suspicious of, if not downright hostile to, autodidacticism. I believe in education; it's why I'm studying to be a teacher. However, I also believe that institutions exist to perpetuate class relations, and academia is no exception. I know that until I earn a PhD, if I ever am able to do so, there are some "experts" who simply will never take anything I have to say seriously.

Regardless of this, I am confident in my knowledge of the subject at hand. I have pondered over Jesus for most of my life, and since discovering the study of him as a historical person I have immersed myself in the material with a fervor and intensity that I daresay is rarely seen among those not working on dissertations or professionally as academics.

PREFACE

I have preemptively defended my right to write this book because I believe in it. I believe that I have something important to say; that this perspective I have on Jesus is worth sharing. The reasons why I believe this will be made clear by the end. For now, to all those who think that only those who've spent decades sitting in plush chairs in universities should write books like this, I implore you to understand that you have been lied to. I invite you to consider that the reason this attitude persists is that it benefits the entrenched and ensures that anything that might challenge long-held notions from outside the clubhouse receives no quarter.

My hope is that this book will challenge some of those notions, both among the faithful laity curious about Jesus as well as the learned clergy. I hope that my argument will be considered on its merits rather than my background. Most of all, I hope that this can contribute to a process of opening the door to a more open form of academia, a proletarian academia that recognizes the intelligence and perspectives of people who cannot afford university educations. Millions of people with brilliant minds languish in poverty all over the world, people much smarter and much worse-off than I. They deserve the space to contribute to the advancement of human thought and knowledge without being disregarded because they haven't read the correct books.

Note that all passages from Scripture, unless otherwise noted, come from the New Revised Standard Version.

ACKNOWLEDGMENTS

I must first and foremost acknowledge the patience, love, and support of my wife, Sara, who has shouldered many of the burdens of everyday life while I've stayed up long nights reading academic journals and trying to get the words to this book out. None of this would be possible without her.

I am indebted to all of the scholars who have contributed to the ongoing Quest for the Historical Jesus, but most especially the work of John Dominic Crossan, whose insights and passionate blend of history and theology formed the basis for my first comprehensive understanding of the historical Jesus, and who has taken the time to answer several borderline-sycophantic emails from me over the years. Even when I think Crossan has gotten something wrong, I have to admit he's wrong for the right reasons.

I also could not have done this without the encouragement and support of my friend Charley Earp, the one and only Commie Preacher, who challenges me on all the right fronts.

Thanks also to Jennifer Gates, Gibson DelGiudice, and Gabe Galloway for being among the first to read and offer valuable criticism.

A special thanks to Tamber Hausler, my partner-in-crime with Red Star Ministry and a lasting inspiration to continue preaching the revolutionary gospel of Jesus.

Finally, I must acknowledge the patience and generosity of all of my black and brown and poor and LGBT and women and disabled comrades, who shoulder the burden of checking my privilege for me and ensuring that I always remember who and what I'm fighting for. There has never been a better group of ragtag misfits hell-bent on changing the world for the better than the current generation of revolutionaries.

INTRODUCTION

A specter is haunting America—the specter of Jesus.

Jesus Christ is a figure of religion and mythology. Miraculous deeds, divine attributes, and arcane sayings are attributed to him, and his billions of followers across the world hold countless views about who he was, what he said, what he meant, and how exactly he was related to God.

Jesus of Nazareth is a figure of history, a real man who lived and died in first-century Palestine, but whose biographical details often seem frustratingly elusive, obscured by the sensational aspects of his religious persona.

Jesus occupies a contradictory place in Western liberal society—our cultural and political institutions have been undeniably shaped by Christianity, and yet we are also an increasingly secularized people. While everyone in the United States knows at least a little about Jesus, relatively few (even among the devout) know much about who he was as a historical person.

There are complex reasons for this, chief among them the fact that the historical man known as Jesus of Nazareth has been divinized and deified for nearly two thousand years by billions of Christians and their institutions. The influence that the Christian religion has had on Western society and culture is almost unimaginably enormous, and so its orthodoxy and dogmas are ubiquitous.

For the interested layperson, there is a surfeit of popular books, many of which were written by knowledgeable secular scholars, about the historical Jesus. Some of these books are very good (and some are less so) but what they all share in common, to their detriment, is that nearly all were written by a community of bourgeois academics and intellectuals, and even the best of them are fettered in many ways by academic jargon, obscure and unfamiliar historical methods, or, at a minimum, the middle- and upper-class background of their authors.

INTRODUCTION

This stands in sharp contrast to the fact that Jesus of Nazareth was a destitute proletarian, a member of the underclass of the society in which he lived. Even the best-intentioned and most correct of these scholars are constrained by the class privileges and concerns of the intelligentsia, and so their analyses are unable to capture the whole of who Jesus really was.

It is high time that Jesus, the man whose revolutionary ministry would change the entire course of human history, is given a biography that reflects his own class background. To this end, I shall undertake the task of creating a proletarian reconstruction of the historical Jesus of Nazareth (both of those words—*proletarian* and *reconstruction*—will be given further explanation soon). I shall analyze the available evidence and argue that it clearly shows that Jesus of Nazareth was a revolutionary whose life, teachings, and death suggest a politics of radical emancipation that can be applied to the twenty-first-century struggle against all forms of exploitation, including white supremacy, patriarchy, imperialism, and capitalism.

Chapter 1

FOUNDATION

And when Pilate, at the suggestion of the principal men amongst us, had condemned him to the cross, those that believed in him did not give up their affection for him.

—JOSEPHUS

OVERTURE: THE CARPENTER'S SON

Nazareth was a village so tiny its very name may have been lost to history if not for the boy who came from there to change the world. It stood only a few miles from Sepphoris, the largest Greek city in Galilee, but its inhabitants were Jews.

This boy looked like the rest of his people: dark skin, dark eyes, even darker hair. The oldest of several children, Jesus learned his father's trade and became a *tekton*. Growing up he became known around his village as *the carpenter's son*.

When the carpenter's son was very young, perhaps an infant, Herod the Great, the King of the Jews and friend of the Romans, died, and rebellions sprouted up all over Palestine, including Galilee. Sepphoris was sacked, first by a bandit revolutionary named Judas and then again by the Romans, who destroyed much of it. For the peasants and day laborers in rural Galilee, the memory of the Roman Legion coming to their land and destroying the large city within walking distance stayed fresh and brutal for decades to come. They told it to their children, to teach them a lesson: this is who the Romans are; this is what the Romans do; this is what happens if you dare oppose them.

Order was restored under Herod Antipas, the son of the former Herod, who rebuilt Sepphoris as "The Ornament of Galilee."[1] This rebuilding project would be good work for *tektons* from the villages surrounding Sepphoris, and the carpenter's son would spend many days in his youth walking there with his father and building the structures that housed the people, both Jews and Gentiles alike, who lived there.

Like all good Jewish boys, the carpenter's son spent as much time as possible at Nazareth's tiny synagogue, an informal common building where the villagers sat or stood in a circle so that they could all see each other while they discussed the Law and the Prophets, and learned the history of his people. This was a time when Jewish practice was heavily centralized at the temple in Jerusalem, and *rabbi* was a word that could describe any Jew who was wise in the teachings of Scripture. The carpenter's son was not able to visit the temple more than once a year for the Passover Festival, so daily religious life centered around this tiny village synagogue.

Carpenter's sons were not afforded the privilege of literacy, but that did not stop this boy from learning everything he could about God, the law of Moses, the people and land of Israel, and the words of the prophets. Devoted and passionate, with a natural, but rugged intelligence, the carpenter's son impressed and astounded his neighbors with his quick grasp of their religious heritage, not to mention his wit.

At some point, the carpenter's son lost his father and he became a man, the *pater* of his family, responsible for his mother and brothers and sisters. He was no longer the carpenter's son; now he was the carpenter.

Life continued in Nazareth, which is to say that it continued to be desperate and alienating. The stories of Israel told of God's unwavering commitment to his people, and yet their king, Herod Antipas, paid tribute every year to a foreign, pagan emperor. While Galilee had a half-Jewish ruler, the tetrarch of Judea, where Jerusalem and the temple were located, was so inept and so brutal that he was expelled and the area came under direct Roman rule when the carpenter's son was still young. These Romans agitated against God by parading graven images in the holy city of Jerusalem, and even threatening to display them at the temple.

1. Josephus, *Antiquities of the Jews*, XVIII.2.

Closer to home, more and more devout Jews had lost or were losing the land that had been promised them by God. Usurers, both Jewish and pagan, flaunted the law of Moses by collecting property through foreclosure to consolidate land and enrich the tiny ruling class that ran society. Unfathomable wealth existed next to harrowing destitution, and this inequality was enforced through cruelty and brutality. All throughout the hills of Galilee, desperate peasants without land, just like the carpenter's son and his family, took to banditry in quixotic protest of their harsh conditions.

The carpenter's son could have become one of them, and may have ended up on a cross much sooner than he eventually did. But he did not. He continued to study the Scriptures, continued to support his family, and took in all that was happening around him. He knew it was unjust. He knew it was profane. But he also remembered those stories about Judas the rebel, and what had happened the last time people had taken up arms en masse against the Roman juggernaut. He saw the mutilated bodies of his neighbors and countrymen, hung on crosses in defiance of torah, denied the honor of a proper burial, their flesh consumed by carrion birds and wild dogs. What could mere men do against such systemic injustice? Why did God not act to free his people?

And then came a voice, crying out in the wilderness. A man named John had gathered followers on the banks of the Jordan river, and this John had initiated a radical new rite of baptism that he said would cleanse people of sins, independently of the corrupt temple in Jerusalem. John's crimes could get him killed, but his message met the ears of the masses, and the Jewish collaborators became too afraid of their wrath to move against John, for the time being.

This was the movement the carpenter's son had been waiting for. He left his family to join John in the wilderness, and his devotion to the cause combined with his intelligence and knowledge of Scripture helped him to rise to a place of prominence within John's apocalyptic movement.

That is what it had become: apocalyptic. God would surely act soon to smite the imperialists from the land he had promised to his people, along with the collaborators. But his people had become unclean, because the institution designed to help them remain pure—the temple—had itself become corrupt. When enough Jews came to the Jordan to be baptized by John, then surely it would happen. John and his followers, including the carpenter's son, believed this.

Finally, John's antics became too much for the country's rulers to bear. He was arrested and thrown in jail, but his popularity among the people kept his head on his shoulders, for the time being. To Herod's consternation, John's followers were undeterred, and many of them assumed temporary leadership roles during John's absence. One of these leaders was the carpenter's son, from Nazareth.

John's movement vexed Herod and his retainers. It was profoundly, radically revolutionary, promising the end of Herod's rule as well as the Romans' dominion over Palestine. And yet, despite the dozens upon dozens of rebels past, present, and future who claimed to be messiahs come to liberate their people, John's movement was nonviolent. And yet unlike other nonviolent movements, the arrest of John had not dulled the passions of his followers. In fact, it only seemed to further embolden them.

Finally, it could not be put off any longer. John, who had continued to prophesy from his prison cell, had to be put to death. He was beheaded on the orders of Herod Antipas, tetrarch of Galilee. Many people were enraged and saddened, and the memory of the charismatic preacher on the banks of the Jordan would endure for decades to come. But John's execution did not spur revolution. More importantly, and more shockingly, neither did it spur divine intervention.

John's followers pondered this. Many lost heart and returned home. Others resolved to continue John's work, baptizing and preaching the imminent coming of the kingdom. One small subsect, led by the carpenter's son, took a third path.

It was apparent to them that John had not been wrong about the corruption of the temple. Nor had he been wrong that God was on the side of his people against imperialism and oppression. Where John had gone wrong was in his method, and this was evidenced by the fact that God had not acted and continued to not act.

The carpenter's son and those who thought like him envisioned a different type of apocalypse, one that they could enact in the name of God without waiting around for a divine intervention that wasn't coming. They broke radically from John: where John was an ascetic, rarely eating or drinking to emphasize that the material world was passing away, they would eat and drink freely, with everyone they came across, to emphasize the primacy of the material world that God had created and the place of the kingdom within it. Where John created a sort of "alternative temple" on the banks of the Jordan, waiting for pilgrims to come to him, they would take the kingdom of God on the road with them, traveling to the poor villages of Galilee and proclaiming its arrival wherever they went. Where John taught that God would wipe away the evil forces of oppression, the carpenter's son and his followers took it upon themselves to do so, by making those powers irrelevant.

The carpenter's son returned to Nazareth to bring his vision of a radically changed society, but was spurned. Undaunted, he continued throughout Galilee, performing signs and wonders for all who would receive him. He proclaimed them clean of ritual impurity; he exorcised the demons that plagued their minds through the force of his charisma and fellowship; he shared food and drink and company with the most oppressed and marginalized people wherever he went. He won as many enemies as he did converts, but tales of this miracle-worker spread throughout the villages of Galilee, and the carpenter's son became known as a prophet, a magician, a rabbi, a miracle-worker. He even earned the respect and support of his mother and siblings.

While he did these things, he created another innovation: he sent his followers out, two-by-two, to do what he did. This movement was not about one man, nor could it have been. The kingdom of God was everywhere, as long as there were people there willing to enact its radical egalitarianism. How, then, could it be confined to the travels of a single prophet? It was everywhere, and so they had to be everywhere.

This continued for some time, until the carpenter's son decided to take his followers to Jerusalem for Passover. Passover was always a charged atmosphere, with pilgrims swarming Jerusalem from hundreds of miles away, many of them in states of religious fervor. The Roman authorities, along with the temple collaborators, had learned to be on high alert for any instances of disturbance.

However, the carpenter's son could not contain his rage at the flagrant displays of commerce taking place at the temple which was supposed to be the holiest place in all creation. Perhaps he planned this demonstration in advance; perhaps he was taken with a sudden prophetic rage. Whatever the case, the carpenter's son and his followers stormed the temple, overturning the cages of the commodified sacrificial animals, driving out the money-changers and usurers, and demonstrating against the center of religious and political corruption and imperial collaboration in the Jewish homeland.

This was more than enough for Pontius Pilate, the Roman governor of Judea, to hastily sign execution orders on this nobody from Nazareth.

The carpenter's son did not have the mass base of support in Jerusalem as he did in Galilee, and he was quickly captured and sent to a cross to die next to other troublemakers. There was no trial, there was no mass outcry to have him either killed or pardoned; there was only the cruel, efficient bureaucracy of state violence.

The death of its founder may have been the end of this movement, as it had been the end of so many others. Instead, something else happened. A miracle.

As one historian would write several decades later of the carpenter's son, "Those who had believed in him did not give up their affection for him." All the lowly people he had met during his time preaching and prophesying in Galilee remembered how it had felt to sit and eat with such a compassionate, well-respected man. The outcast and marginalized, especially the women, remembered that he had accepted them, had embraced them, as an equal. The sick and disabled remembered how the carpenter's son had declared them clean, forgiven, and pure. And those who had been with him at the end remembered the resolution with which he accepted and faced his own death, assured that he had taught his followers well enough to carry on without him.

Unlike John's movement, and unlike countless other movements whose leaders have been lost to history, the followers of the carpenter's son continued their work after his death. They continued to travel, continued to heal the sick and exorcise demons and proclaim the good news to the poor and downtrodden. And when they spoke of the carpenter's son, they spoke not of a dead man, but of a man who continued to abide with them, a man whose presence they still felt in the sharing of a meal with strangers.

Jesus of Nazareth was dead. The faith called Christianity had only just begun.

THE JESUS OF HISTORY

The preceding section is, of course, dramatized. It is my best estimation at a historically accurate (as well as highly condensed) biography of the man called Jesus of Nazareth, who walked the land of Palestine in the first century of the Common Era. It is placed at the beginning of this book so that you, the reader, know exactly what you are getting into.

If you are a Christian or familiar with Christian mythology,[2] you were probably immediately struck by the things that were missing from that short biography. Where was the virgin birth in Bethlehem? The trial before Pilate? The empty tomb?

Allow me to introduce you to a man and a concept called *The Jesus of History*. This is a term used often by scholars to distinguish the actual, historical Jesus of Nazareth from what is often termed "The Christ of Faith." These two concepts—Jesus of History, Christ of Faith—form a dialectic that many Christian scholars, both progressive and conservative, have grappled with in various ways. Christians all over the world worship an idea—Jesus as God, Son of God, and Messiah—and the vast majority of them assume that this concept is identical with the real, flesh-and-blood man who walked the earth in first-century Palestine. To suggest otherwise would be blasphemy to them.

Historians both Christian and non-Christian, however, have thought differently for centuries. The first "Quest for the Historical Jesus" began during the eighteenth century, when academics and intellectuals questioned the historical veracity of the gospel accounts of the life of Jesus. This quest lasted until Albert Schweitzer published *The Quest of the Historical Jesus* in 1906. Schweitzer, a Christian, expertly criticized many past attempts to historicize Jesus and concluded that the historical Jesus was and would remain out of reach.

The "Second Quest" began in the 1950s, and introduced many methodological approaches that have since become staples of this type of work, such as the "criterion of embarrassment"[3] and the "criterion of dissimilarity."[4]

The current "Third Quest" began in the 1980s with the Jesus Seminar, and has focused on rigorous textual criticism, including source criticism. Basically, scholars active in this Quest begin with the distinct sources underlying the gospels, and try to assess their reliability using various methods.

---

2. Right off the bat, you should know that I do not mean the word "mythology" derisively or pejoratively. It does not equate to "false."

3. If an event or saying is something that would have embarrassed the early Christians, it is more likely to have been authentic, because they would have had less reason to invent or embellish it.

4. This holds that the more dissimilar a saying of Jesus is to contemporary Jewish or early Christian thought, the more likely it is to be authentic. This one is controversial and, in my opinion, of limited use. (It presupposes that Jesus broke from the Judaism of his time, a claim which must be demonstrated based on evidence first.)

What scholars and historians throughout all three quests have attempted to do is to "reconstruct" the historical Jesus. The prefix *re-* is important because by definition, all of these scholars begin with the Christ of Faith—Jesus as he is presented in the Christian New Testament, taken at face value—and then subtract elements until they are left with only what is as close to historically certain as we can ever hope to be. Then they proceed to build upon that initial foundation using whatever methods they believe are best. Some reconstructions are scarce and barren, blasphemous to most Christians, while others are very lackadaisical and seem to conform to the scholar's religious presuppositions (these are usually done by religiously conservative Christian scholars).

So we understand what a *reconstruction* is. But what about that other word I promised I would elaborate upon? *Proletarian?*

While I have a great amount of respect for many scholars active today in the Third Quest for the Historical Jesus, I do not place this book among the Third Quest. This Third Quest is stuck, may in fact be coming to an end, with no new revelations or revolutions in years.[5]

Each quest for the historical Jesus has seen great advances in its methodology and treatment of its subject, in many cases helped by new archaeological discoveries such as the Dead Sea Scrolls and the Nag Hammadi Library. My reconstruction will take the best parts of all of these former works, but apply them within a different framework. I am going to take a historical materialist approach to reconstructing Jesus.

Most Americans are familiar with the term *proletariat* from Marxist thought. The proletariat is the working class, the class of people who do not own property or capital and must survive by selling their labor to the capitalist/bourgeoisie class.

Historical materialism is the Marxist approach to history. It treats history as a march forward, advancing through various epochs in different times and places through class struggle. It also sees a society's culture, including religion, politics, beliefs, customs, art, and much more, as emerging from its *economic base*—that's the class structure of that society: who owns what, who produces what, and most importantly, who profits. As Engels put it:

---

5. The last great splash may have been Reza Aslan's *Zealot*, published in 2013, and yet even *Zealot*, for all the mainstream attention it received, did not advance any brand-new hypotheses.

> *According to [historical materialism], the determining factor in history is, in the final instance, the production and reproduction of the immediate essentials of life. This, again, is of a twofold character. On the one side, the production of the means of existence, of articles of food and clothing, dwellings, and of the tools necessary for that production; on the other side, the production of human beings themselves, the propagation of the species. The social organization under which the people of a particular historical epoch and a particular country live is determined by both kinds of production: by the stage of development of labor on the one hand and of the family on the other.*[6]

This is important for understanding *proletarian*. In addition to its use in Marxist theory, it also had a specific meaning in Roman times, during the time of Jesus. The Roman census listed all citizens along with their property, most importantly land and livestock (the capital of an agrarian economy). Citizens without property, however, listed their children instead. *Prole* means "offspring" and these proletarians were valued for their ability to produce future Romans.

Jesus was not a Roman citizen, and so he was not literally a proletarius. The gospels do list his occupation, however, as a *tekton*, a builder or carpenter. While Americans may think of carpentry as a skilled craft begetting a middle-class lifestyle, in an agrarian slave economy, it meant that you were poor and owned no land of your own. It was a comparatively small class, but it existed, as it does today, in a state of perpetual precarity, selling its labor to the owners of capital to survive. In the larger sense, the Marxist sense, Jesus of Nazareth was every bit a proletarian as the working class of the twenty-first century.

Few scholars of the historical Jesus understand this fundamental fact. When they do acknowledge it, they miss its full implications because they lack a materialist analysis of history. This is to be expected as the academic community is overwhelmingly bourgeois, if not in their direct relationship to capital, then certainly in their thought. I will demonstrate how any accurate and meaningful reconstruction of Jesus must be thoroughly proletarian in nature, because seeing Jesus through a proletarian lens is seeing him through his own lens.

If you are a Christian and have read this far, you may be uncomfortable. I have, after all, suggested to you that some of the things you believe

---

6. Engels, *Origin of the Family*, 35.

about the man you call God are, at the very least, not historical. Some may even be that dreaded W-word, *wrong*.

I urge you to embrace this contradiction between the Jesus of History and the Christ of Faith. Recognize it as a contradiction. If the two are distinct—if the concept Christians worship as God, the Son of God, the Messiah, is different somehow than the actual, real person upon which the idea is based—well, what does that say about Christianity?

We will get to the bottom of that question, and I posit that Christianity will be enriched for it. Do not be afraid of contradiction. "Every difference in men's concepts should be regarded as reflecting an objective contradiction. Objective contradictions are reflected in subjective thinking, and this process . . . pushes forward the development of thought, and ceaselessly solves problems in man's thinking."[7]

PRESUPPOSITIONS AND SOURCES

This will not, and indeed can not, be a truly exhaustive tome on the historical Jesus. I do not expect it will be the only book I write on the historical Jesus. I could write a million words on the subject and still have more to say. To save on time, I will begin by clearly laying out the presuppositions which will guide my reconstruction.

The first I have already discussed. I am a Marxist and a materialist. I believe that "there is nothing in this world except matter in motion"[8] and I believe that nearly everything about human society is downstream from what we'd call "economics." Fulfilling our material needs comes first, and the way(s) in which we do it conditions everything else.

Historical materialism, once grasped, is so self-evident that it scarcely need be argued for at all. Be that as it may, that is not the purpose of this book. I believe that the proof will be in the pudding, as it were, and that the fruit of this endeavor will be as strong an argument for historical materialism as any philosophical tome. In any case, because it is the framework I will be using to reconstruct the historical Jesus, I do not feel the need to spend time discussing it other than to explain it, which I have.

Next, and related, is that I do not believe in miracles or the supernatural. I am a Christian, and so I treat the stories of the supernatural and

---

7. Mao Zedong, *On Contradiction*, ch. 2, lines 22–23.
8. Mao Zedong, *On Contradiction*, ch. 2, lines 22–23.

divine within the Bible very seriously. However, I do not believe that they actually happened.

Some scholars of the historical Jesus treat this issue quite dishonestly, considering the supernatural claims in the gospels simply as pericopes to be weighed against the textual evidence, and then either counted or discounted on an individual basis. This is wrong. It is not the job of a historian to disprove something unfalsifiable, much less something that is physically and scientifically impossible to the best of our available knowledge. The burden of proof for the historicity of a supernatural occurrence is on the one who wishes to prove it.

To be clear, I am not saying that I will ignore the stories of supernatural happenings. They will be considered as events that the authors of the gospels truly believed happened, and given the full weight of that reality. What I *am* saying is that I will discount stories of a man changing water into wine, walking on the sea, and casting out demons as being *literally and factually true* because you cannot turn water into wine; humans cannot walk on the sea; and demons don't exist. If this offends your religious sensibilities, all I can do is shrug and move on.

Next, with little exception, I accept the consensus of New Testament scholars about the sources of the gospels and their usefulness for reconstructing a historical Jesus. Because most lay readers are likely to be unfamiliar with this, I will discuss this at some length.

While it comes second in the New Testament, the Gospel of Mark is almost certainly the earliest of the four canonical gospels. I favor a date just after 70 CE, during or just after the First Roman-Jewish War, which ended with the destruction of Jerusalem and the second temple.

Mark, Matthew, and Luke form what are called the *Synoptic* Gospels—which means "seen together." This is because they share a great many similarities, as contrasted with the Gospel of John, which is quite different. The reason for these similarities is that Matthew and Luke probably used Mark as the basis of their own gospel, along with another source nicknamed Q (for *quelle*, German for "source.")

We know this because in addition to copying most of Mark's narrative, both Matthew and Luke contain many elements found in each other, but not Mark. This material is believed to originate from a *sayings* gospel which has since been lost to history. This is called the two-source theory, and it is important to note that in this theory, Matthew and Luke are independent of each other; that is, the author of Matthew did not know about Luke's gospel, and the author of Luke did not know about Matthew's gospel. Instead, they both created similar (although distinct in many ways) gospels using the same two sources.

There is an alternative theory, sometimes called the Farrer Hypothesis, which posits that Luke knew both Matthew and Mark and based his gospel on them. I find this theory unconvincing. Its greatest strength is that it does not rely on a hypothetical sayings gospel, but this argument has lost most of its weight since the discovery of the *Gospel of Thomas*, which is a very early sayings gospel. It also does not account for significant differences between Luke and Matthew, or for Luke's preference for Mark's wording of most passages over Matthew's, or for the primitivity of Luke's versions of certain sayings (such as the Lord's Prayer).

So for my reconstruction, I take Mark and Q as two distinct, early sources for the sayings and deeds and stories attributed to Jesus in the gospels. This, again, is by a healthy majority the opinion of most New Testament scholars.

Another important early source is the aforementioned *Gospel of Thomas*. It is a short sayings gospel, which I and numerous other scholars judge independent of the Synoptic Gospels in its original form.[9]

Other early Christian writings that may occasionally prove useful (although are never taken as proof of authenticity on their own) are the *Didache*, a sort of early Christian manual of practice; the "epistle" of James, a collection of sayings originating with Jesus's brother James; and the seven authentic letters of Paul—Romans, both Corinthians, 1 Thessalonians, Galatians, Philippians, and Philemon.

You may be wondering where the Gospel of John fits in all of this. The answer is nowhere. The scholarly consensus is that John was written in the second century CE. It may or may not have drawn from the earlier gospels, but in any case, the vast majority of its traditions are completely unique to it. With apologies to its many fans (of which I count myself one), the Gospel of John is of very little use for this type of historical work. I take most of its traditions and sayings as nonhistorical. The rare occasion that there is a parallel between John and the synoptic tradition will be noted.

This talk of sources and dating and interdependence (or lack thereof) of documents is important because a historical reconstruction of Jesus

---

9. See esp. Patterson, *Thomas and Christian Origins*, and DeConick, "Gospel of Thomas." Other important scholars taking this position include John Dominic Crossan, Uta Ranke-Heinemann, Gerd Theissen, Claus-Hunno Hunzinger, and Helmut Koester.

involves sifting through dozens upon dozens of small units of story—a saying, a miracle, a narrative, a parable—called *pericopes*—and weighing them against the evidence. One of the most important pieces of evidence is that of multiple independent attestation. If two or more sources independently agree on a saying of Jesus, it is much more likely to have been something Jesus actually said (as opposed to something the author of the text made up, or something someone else said that got attributed to Jesus later).

The Jesus Seminar made waves in the '80s for a somewhat-gimmicky method of treating these pericopes by voting on them, and then assigning them little colored balls based on the majority opinion of their authenticity. They were either (a) most likely authentic; (b) probably not something Jesus actually said, but consistent with his teachings; and (c) not something he said, and indicative of later thought. While the idea of voting on sayings in this manner does strike one as a bit odd, these categories are useful for thinking of these pericopes. Just because Jesus probably didn't say or do something himself doesn't mean that it is not important or should be thrown away entirely; these sayings were put in his mouth for a reason, after all.

Two non-Christian sources are equally important; they are histories written by the Roman historian Tacitus and the Jewish historian Josephus. Both of these historians mentioned Jesus, each in passing, and the fact that they are ostensibly neutral about him (not themselves being Christians) is hugely important.

Secondarily, I shall use the rest of the Christian Bible (both testaments) as well as other early Jewish or Christian writings, where appropriate, for context.

My approach will not be mechanical. What I mean by this is that I shall not be checking off boxes for each criterion and judging a tradition authentic or not based solely on how many boxes it fills. Each pericope or tradition will be judged on its own merit and used to draw a holistic picture of Jesus.

My final presupposition is the most personal, and it is that faith has nothing to do with "belief." By belief I mean simply, "believing that a statement or doctrine is true." I was a Christian before I learned of the historical Jesus, and I am a Christian after, but for a time in between, I was not certain.

This is important because, as with any reconstruction of Jesus, there will come the inevitable accusation that I am simply projecting my own beliefs onto Jesus. This is a natural critique to make, but it is also wrong. I was a Christian before I was a Marxist or a communist. I understood Jesus as most Christians do, *prima facie* based on the Bible and what priests and ministers told me. When I began studying the historical Jesus, however, I seriously debated for a long time whether or not I could continue to be a Christian.

I felt, as many Christians no doubt may feel while reading this book (if I do my job, that is) that everything I'd believed about Jesus was a lie. I had believed that Jesus was the Son of God; that he was born of a virgin mother; that he walked on the sea and changed water into wine; that he healed the sick; that he rose from the dead; that he had come to save me from my sins. The historical evidence was telling me that all of those things were incorrect. Why, then, be a Christian?

Finally I realized that all of those things were things that I believed *about* Jesus. I refuse to let that be what my faith means. It has nothing to do with what I believe about Jesus—people can believe whatever they want about Jesus—and everything to do with whether or not I believe *in* Jesus. To believe in Jesus means to follow him, to do as he did, to take up his cross and fight for what he fought for. That is what led me down the path to becoming a communist; not the other way around.

You see, hard to believe as it may be, being a communist did not make me see Jesus the way I see him. Understanding Jesus the way I do is what made me into a communist. My goal is that by the end of this book, it shall do the same for you.

JESUS: MAN OR MYTH?

As much as I wish I did not have to do this, we must begin by demonstrating that Jesus actually existed. This is because there is a small, fringe, but vocal group of people who contend loudly and to anyone who will listen that Jesus never existed as a historical person. While this position usually finds favor among reactionary New Atheists, is unfortunately has also found some adherents among the Left as well, and so it must be disposed of.

More positively, you cannot *re*-construct something without first *de*-constructing it. So that is what we must do.

We start with the fact that a religion exists—Christianity—and that it is based upon the life of Jesus Christ, who walked the Earth two millennia ago performing miracles, was crucified by the Roman Empire, and then rose from the dead. The Christians have an entire book—the New

Testament—full of information about this person, so we must know a great deal about him, right?

Not exactly. The one thing that the Jesus mythicists get right is that the gospels cannot be trusted as objective, factual, eyewitness accounts of the life of Jesus. They were clearly written to exalt this man by his own followers, and they contradict each other in far too many ways to be fully harmonized. Perhaps they could still be used to glean information about this man, if he existed, but not on their own.

So we must turn to our other sources first. First are the letters of Paul, who was also a disciple of Jesus and so whose words must be taken with a grain of salt.

Paul's letters deal mostly with concerns that the churches he founded were having and were never intended to even resemble biographies of Jesus. However, he does mention a few things in passing about the man who founded his movement. These are:

- Jesus was born a Jew, a man, to a human mother (Gal 4:4).
- Jesus died by crucifixion (1 Cor 1:23; 2:2; 2:8 ; 2 Cor 13:4).
- Jesus was (allegedly) a descendent of King David (Rom 1:3).
- Jesus was also, as with all Jews, a descendent of Abraham (Gal 3:16).
- Jesus left teachings on subjects such as the coming apocalypse (1 Thess 4:15) and divorce (1 Cor 7:10).
- Jesus had multiple brothers (1 Cor 9:5).
- One of these brothers was named James (Gal 1:19).

Again, however, this evidence is scant and inconclusive at best. What it tells us is that Paul, writing in the 50s and 60s CE (about twenty to thirty years after Jesus supposedly died) certainly believed that Jesus had been a real, flesh-and-blood man who had walked the earth and instituted the religious movement that Paul now followed.

Next we turn to our best non-Christian source, Josephus. Josephus was a Jewish-Roman historian and aristocrat who defected to Rome during the First Roman-Jewish War and ingratiated himself with the future emperor Vespasian. He wrote a twenty-volume history of the Jewish people called *Antiquities of the Jews*, or *Antiquities* for short. This text mentions Jesus twice, in volumes 18 and 20.

The first reference, in volume 18, is called the Testimonium Flavianum. Our earliest version of Antiquities dates from the eleventh century, and this section (18:63–64) reads:

> Now there was about this time Jesus, a wise man, if it be lawful to call him a man; for he was a doer of mysterious deeds, a teacher of such men as receive the truth with pleasure. He drew over to him both many of the Jews and many of the Gentiles. He was [the] Christ. And when Pilate, at the suggestion of the principal men amongst us, had condemned him to the cross, those that loved him at the first did not forsake him; for he appeared to them alive again the third day; as the divine prophets had foretold these and ten thousand other wonderful things concerning him. And the tribe of Christians, so named from him, are not extinct at this day.

If that reads a bit too good to be true, that's because it is. Josephus's works were copied and preserved throughout much of the millennium between its composition and our earliest manuscript by Christians, and these Christians could not help but make some "improvements" to what Josephus wrote. Here is the likely original version:

> Now there was about this time Jesus, a wise man. He was a doer of mysterious deeds, a teacher of such men as receive the truth with pleasure. He drew over to him both many of the Jews and many of the Gentiles. He was called [emphasis mine] Christ. And when Pilate, at the suggestion of the principal men amongst us, had condemned him to the cross, those that believed in him did not give up their affection for him. And the tribe of Christians, so named from him, are not extinct at this day.

Jesus mythicists generally argue, against the consensus of most experts of this history, that the entire passage is an interpolation (added later) and not even this historical core is original. Their evidence for this claim is basically nonexistent, while the evidence for the passage's authenticity is overwhelming:

- It utilizes language characteristic of Josephus, such as:
    - "Now there was about this time," a phrase Josephus uses regularly to introduce a new event or idea in his works;
    - Jesus is described as a "wise man" (σοφὸς ἀνήρ, *sophós anír*). This phrase is never used to describe Jesus in any early Christian

writings, nor does it exist in the Synoptic Gospels. Josephus also uses it to describe the prophet Daniel in book 10 of *Antiquities*.

> Jesus's miracles are described as "mysterious [literally *paradoxical*] deeds" (παραδόξων ἔργων, *paradoxon ergon*), a neutral phrase that is likewise never used in any Christian writings to refer to the miracles of Jesus, yet is also used by Josephus to refer to the deeds of Eliseus (Elisha) in *Antiquities*, book 9.

> Christians are described as a "tribe" or "people" (φῦλον, *phylon*). No early Christian writings ever refer to the Christian community as a whole in this way, but Josephus uses it frequently.

- The second-century Christian writer Origen specifically mentions in *Against Celsus* that Josephus did not believe in Jesus "as the Messiah." That would be a very strange thing to say if Josephus had never mentioned Jesus at all.[10] Origen repeats this claim in book 10 of his commentary on Matthew, as well as quoting Josephus's other reference to Jesus (more on that below).
- The Testimonium is actually required for Josephus's second reference to Jesus, in book 20, to make sense.

So we turn now to that second reference. It is much shorter and simpler than the first. The relevant portion reads: "[Ananus the high priest] assembled the sanhedrin of judges, and brought before them James, the brother of Jesus, who was called Christ, and some of his companions, and when he had formed an accusation against them as breakers of the law, he delivered them to be stoned."

This is in the context of political turmoil following the death of Festus, the procurator of Judea, in 62 CE. The high priest Ananus took advantage of the power vacuum between Festus's death and the arrival of his successor (Albinus) from Rome to have "James, the brother of Jesus, who was called Christ" executed, along with some others (who were probably also Christians).

This James is almost certainly who Christians refer to as James the Just, who led the earliest Christian community in Jerusalem after the death of Jesus. This James was also Jesus's brother, which is corroborated by Paul's

---

10. Christians were not in any position to be altering Josephan manuscripts during the time of Origen, so any interpolations would have to have come from much later than he was writing.

reference to "James, the brother of the Lord" in Galatians (see above). This second reference to Jesus, from book 20, is nearly universally regarded as authentic and not an interpolation by Josephan scholars.[11]

This second reference, which again is universally regarded as authentic to Josephus, only makes sense if Josephus had previously referred to Jesus and his title as Christ. It is characteristic of his writing (and other historians of the era) when referring to a person with a common name to differentiate them by mentioning a relative, such as "son of" or "brother of." So "James, the brother of Jesus, who was called Christ" makes the most sense if Josephus had previously referred to a "Jesus who was called Christ."

I could continue beating this point into the ground, but others have done so better than I could hope to, and it would take over the rest of this book. Indeed, entire books have been written methodically picking apart the entire idea that Jesus never existed.[12] What I have tried to do here is lay out the reasons that Josephus's references to Jesus can be considered reliable, because (a) we will be using them to lay the foundation for our reconstruction, and (b) to introduce newer readers to some of the types of critical issues that are at play here. If you are truly stuck on whether or not there even was a historical Jesus, for now I will have to be content with urging you to read on with an open mind, consider my reconstruction, and see if it isn't a reasonable explanation for how Christianity might have emerged.[13]

THE NON-CHRISTIAN SOURCES

A reconstruction is only as strong as the foundation upon which it stands. Because of my desire to create as accurate a reconstruction as possible, we will use non-Christian sources for our foundation.

---

11. Even the ever-present Richard Carrier cannot deny that it is authentic to the text; he gets around this with a ludicrous argument that only the phrase "who was called Christ" is an interpolation, and that the Jesus in question is a different Jesus. This is not supported whatsoever by the text.

12. Bart Ehrman's *Did Jesus Exist?* is the best of them.

13. That, and to visit the website *History for Atheists*, which has the finest collection of anti-mythicist writing I've yet encountered. Tim O'Neill, who is himself an ardent atheist, savagely debunks all of the arguments against the existence of a historical Jesus and expertly makes the case that his existence is all but historically certain (https://historyforatheists.com/).

The main non-Christian source, as previously discussed, is Josephus. Added to this is a scant reference from Tacitus, a Roman historian, from the early second century CE.

While many historians consider the *Testimonium Flavianum*'s statement that Jesus "was the Christ" to be an interpolation, for reasons previously discussed, I find this unlikely. Because of the second reference, to James the brother of Jesus who was called Christ, it is more likely that Josephus originally mentioned Jesus's messianic status, but in a neutral way, the way a reporter might. Here is the likely original text of the Testimonium again:

> *Now there was about this time Jesus, a wise man. He was a doer of mysterious deeds, a teacher of such men as receive the truth with pleasure. He drew over to him both many of the Jews and many of the Gentiles. He was called Christ. And when Pilate, at the suggestion of the principal men amongst us, had condemned him to the cross, those that believed in him did not give up their affection for him. And the tribe of Christians, so named from him, are not extinct at this day.*

This short passage tells us a fair amount of information just from a surface-level reading, but a true materialist reading takes into account the historical context as well as the class background of the author. Most of the succeeding information comes from his own accounts of his life, a fact which should be kept in mind at all times.

Flavius Josephus was a wealthy, aristocratic Jewish historian who betrayed his own people to cozy up to a Roman emperor. While commanding the Jewish forces in Galilee against the Romans, Josephus found himself and several dozen of his comrades under siege, trapped in a cave by the Roman military. According to his own account, Josephus suggested a mass suicide to his followers rather than be captured by the Romans; when most of them were dead, he himself surrendered and offered his services as an interpreter to the Romans.

Apparently, Josephus flattered the Roman general, Flavius Vespasian, by claiming to have received a revelation from God that Vespasian would become emperor of Rome and that Rome had been ordained by God to punish the Jews. At least the first half of this "revelation" turned out to be true, as Vespasian became emperor in 69 CE. Vespasian freed Josephus and Josephus eventually settled in Rome, where he continued to be close with Vespasian's family, serving his son Titus when he succeeded the throne.

The *Antiquities*—written in Rome around the turn of the second century—is a comprehensive explication of the history and significance of the Jewish people, from Creation until the time Josephus was writing (about 94 CE). Its target audience was probably Greek-speaking Gentiles throughout the Empire who had an interest in Judaism, either because they governed cities with large diaspora populations or out of sheer religious curiosity. Very few people in antiquity were literate enough to be able to read such a volume, so the elite (scribes, politicians, the wealthy) classes of Rome are primarily who Josephus was writing for.

It is important to keep these biases in mind as we take from Josephus's testimony to build our foundation.

In addition, we will consider the aforementioned account of Tacitus. In the *Annals*, book 15, v. 44, Tacitus writes of the Great Fire of Rome, which occurred in 64 CE under Emperor Nero. According to Tacitus, Nero was blamed by many influential people for intentionally starting the fire, and to escape condemnation, sought a scapegoat:

> *Consequently, to get rid of the report, Nero fastened the guilt and inflicted the most exquisite tortures on a class hated for their abominations, called Christians[14] by the populace. Christ, from whom the name had its origin, suffered the extreme penalty during the reign of Tiberius at the hands of one of our procurators, Pontius Pilatus, and a most mischievous superstition, thus checked for the moment, again broke out not only in Judea, the first source of the evil, but even in Rome, where all things hideous and shameful from every part of the world find their center and become popular.*[15]

Jesus ("Christus") is only mentioned in passing, but this offers a wealth of corroborating information with Josephus, and even the gospel accounts. Tacitus was writing between one and three decades after Josephus, again in Rome, again for a primarily elite, Gentile audience, although Tacitus's contempt for the Christians is blisteringly obvious (elsewhere he makes it clear that he has a general disdain for all Jews as well).

These two non-Christian sources provide us with the most unbiased accounts of the historical Jesus. Tacitus, an anti-Jewish, anti-Christian Gentile historian, widely considered one of the most reliable and meticulous

---

14. The only extant manuscript of this text we have actually reads "Chrestians," but this is either a simple variant spelling or, more likely, a scribal error.

15. For a robust defense of the passage's authenticity, visit https://historyforatheists.com/2017/09/jesus-mythicism-1-the-tacitus-reference-to-jesus/.

historians of his kind; and Josephus, a Jewish, priestly, aristocratic historian who was also a friend to the Romans. Later interpolations (of Josephus) aside, neither of these two had any reason to glorify, exalt, or lie in favor of the Christians or their founder.

From the two of them, we can say with confidence that Jesus was:

- Jewish
- Called "Christ," which means "messiah"
- Executed by Pontius Pilate, in Judea, during the reign of Tiberius (which narrows the timeline down to 27–37 CE)
- Founded a movement that spread throughout the Roman Empire, to Rome itself, among Jews and Gentiles

These passages, taken together also, tell us about the state of Christianity around the turn of the second century CE. Some of this information may be useful to retroject back onto the historical Jesus, but not at this juncture. That will come later, when we briefly look at the trajectory of early Christianity in light of our findings on the historical Jesus.

Before proceeding, we must take a step back. We may now locate Jesus at a specific time—around the year 30 CE—and place, Judea/Palestine. We cannot hope to understand our sources about Jesus, or indeed the man himself, without understanding this time and place.

We also know another crucial factor about Jesus—he was a Jew during the Second Temple Period (which ended when the temple was destroyed in the year 70 CE, as a result of that war Josephus took part in). As a Jew, he was inextricably shaped by the Jewish Scriptures, Jewish culture, and the Jewish experience.

We must now delve into the historical background of the Jewish people, from creation up until the Second Temple Period. Doing so will allow us to make sense of our sources for the life of the historical Jesus.

Chapter 2

HISTORICAL CONTEXT

The history of all hitherto existing societies is the history of class struggle.

—Marx and Engels

MODES OF PRODUCTION

In prehistoric times, before the Neolithic (agricultural) revolution, humans lived in small, nomadic bands or semipermanent settlements. The nomadic bands practiced hunting and gathering to produce the immediate essentials of life, while the small settlements added horticulture into the mix. These are what is referred to as "modes of production."

One defining characteristic of both hunter-gatherer and horticultural societies is that they are extremely egalitarian (or in some cases complementarian). While men and women may have had different roles in the production of essentials and the reproduction of the species, neither had absolute power over the other.[1] Nor were there classes; all people worked as much as their physical and mental ability would allow them to and the food and goods the society produced was shared mostly equally.

---

1. I do not believe in a strict gender binary. This is a simplification and these societies lacked a single defining conception of gender.

These early modes of production (hunting and gathering; horticulture) can provide enough means of subsistence to support small communities, but not the concept of "wealth" or "private property." Wealth / private property is the accumulation of resources by an individual or group beyond what they need to survive. As humans developed the capacity to produce more (by inventing better tools and more complex, productive social relations) we suddenly had to deal with a brand-new problem: we were producing more than we needed.

This marked the turn from horticulture to agriculture. Growing food became more specialized, as instead of maintaining small, community gardens farmers now turned toward larger fields of staple crops. For the first time ever, it became possible to save resources for later, or for one person to live off of the labor of another.

This led to the development of currency, cities, and most importantly, class society. The very first clans to accumulate wealth eventually became the aristocratic classes, leveraging this ownership into social control over others over generations. These classes legitimized themselves through the teaching and maintaining of religious ideas about the universe, the world, and human beings; for example, the Jews believed that God had ordained the priestly class to function as the de facto leaders of the people. Throughout history, all kings and queens have claimed divine mandate for their rule.

Class society is synonymous with inequality. When human societies can only produce enough to feed themselves, it is impossible for one person to hoard resources without the rest of the tribe killing them and taking it back. With agriculture, however, it is possible for one person to produce more than they need. If you have a great harvest but your neighbor's field is destroyed by a pestilence, you have power over that neighbor.

This fact, of some people having more power than others, is what leads to exploitation. If you have something that your neighbor needs to survive (food, or eventually, money) then you can make your neighbor do something for you. Perhaps your neighbor now has to work in your field in exchange for a portion of the harvest; or perhaps they give you a portion of next year's harvest.

This is coupled with the emergence of a division of labor. Whereas in prehistoric modes of production, every member of society did a little bit of everything, now people had defined occupations. Most members of the lower class were farmers, naturally, but with agriculture providing more food than the farmers could themselves eat, new occupations arose, such as professional soldiers, artisans, scribes, and priests. Societies began to form complex social relations, which were always hierarchical. While the farmers produced the vast majority of a society's wealth, most of it was appropriated by the ruling class to finance the building of cities and the creation of standing armies.

A new social class also emerges around this time: the slave. Ancient slavery was different in many important respects from the chattel slavery of more recent history, although it was still inherently exploitative and in many cases brutal.

As the wealthy gained control over more and more of society's wealth (including land), they needed laborers to work it. While there were some free wage laborers (such as Jesus), much of the type of work we'd consider "industrial" (such as manufacturing and construction) was done by slaves.

You could become a slave in one of two ways: either by being sold into slavery as punishment for some crime, or as a result of being conquered by a foreign power.

Many ancient peoples were forced into slavery (or sold their own children into slavery) as a result of debt. The Greek city of Athens faced a debt crisis in the seventh century BCE, as foreclosures on agricultural land forced many peasants into slavery or brigandry.[2]

Conquering foreign peoples was an excellent way to quickly receive an influx of new wealth-generating labor-power; indeed, for much of the Imperial period of Rome's history, this was the primary source of economic growth.

Slavery was seen as a fact of life in the ancient world, but that does not mean that it was not regulated or recognized as unfortunate. The Hebrew Bible regulated slavery, as it did nearly every aspect of life for Jews, in a way that treated it as almost a necessary, but temporary, evil.

It is, however, a mistake to think of "slavery" as the sole or dominant form of labor employed in these types of societies. Slavery coexisted with wage labor, and the vast majority of labor was agricultural, which still involved traditional peasants. Many slaves were kept as stores of value or status symbols, and the slaves of wealthy or powerful people often lived better lives than free poor people (this is in sharp contrast to modern forms

---

2. The crisis was solved when a legislator named Solon instituted sweeping debt and foreclosure reforms and a massive debt forgiveness program.

HISTORICAL CONTEXT

of slavery). Josephus, for example, was an emperor's slave and ended his life as a free man of means serving that same emperor's family.

So the ancient Near Eastern world Judaism developed within was an agricultural class society. Classes are defined by their relationship to a society's means of production. These types of ancient societies basically had two over-classes: producers, including slaves, peasants, and destitute wage laborers, who made up the vast majority of the population; and those who lived off of their labor, such as the aristocracy, clergy, and retainers (such as professional soldiers). Patricians and plebeians, if you will.

But Israel was unique, not just in how they worshiped, but in how they approached the realities of class society.

JUDAISM AND CLASS SOCIETY

A crucial aspect of historical materialism is that the mode of production, which forms the economic base of a society, has a determining[3] influence upon that society's superstructure, or culture. So, for example, in hunter-gatherer or horticultural societies, family ties are loose and egalitarian, because society is communal and property is shared equally. Family lineage is generally matrilineal,[4] which makes sense, as it's hard to be sure of paternity in such a society. As societies advance to agricultural modes of production and become class societies, however, the "traditional family" develops as a vehicle for keeping property within the same lineage.[5] So cultural institutions (like the family) are directly shaped by the economic conditions of the society in which they appear. Keep that in mind as we discuss the Hebrew Bible's teachings on wealth and class society.

The fascinating thing about Judaism is that, even deep into the historical stage of "civilization,"[6] its religious customs preserved remnants of the

---

3. Although not "deterministic," which is a mistake many critics of materialism and even some Marxists make.

4. Knight, "Early Human Kinship."

5. The family and its relation to private property and class society will be discussed in detail later, as Jesus had quite a bit to say about it.

6. I mean "civilization" in a similar sense as the now-outdated three-stage "Savagery-Barbarism-Civilization" understanding of the development of human societies (see Engels, also Lewis Morgan). While this framework is still very useful, it lacks nuance and its former two terms have become quite loaded with negative connotations since it was first conceptualized. "Civilized" is how the Romans saw themselves against the "barbarian" peoples of northern Europe, so it applies here.

egalitarianism that characterized earlier modes of production. The reasons for this will be made clear shortly, but for now let's look at these commandments in the Torah:

- Land could not be sold "in perpetuity." Jews believed that God had given the land to his people, and each family was supposed to own their own piece of ancestral land. Thus, every fifty years, during the Jubilee year, all land was to be returned to its ancestral owner.[7]
- Every seven years (the "Sabbath year") all debts among the Israelites were to be canceled.[8]
- Fellow Israelites who "fell into difficulty" were to be cared for by their neighbors and were not to be charged interest on loans or in any way profited from.[9]
- Lending with interest was absolutely forbidden among Israelites (but allowed to Gentiles).[10]
- Jews were forbidden from reaping the entirety of their fields and explicitly commanded to leave some of it for the poor.[11]

Some of these laws may not seem progressive by the standards of twenty-first-century liberalism (especially in that many of them only applied to Israelites), but for the time, they were extremely radical. Their purpose was not simple charity or alms; as Bible scholar Marcus Borg put it: "The intent is clear: to prevent the growth of a permanently indebted and indentured class . . . to prevent the growth of a permanently landless and impoverished class."[12]

This tendency became even stronger in the next part of the Hebrew Bible, the Prophets or Nevi'im. Many of the "Latter Prophets" harshly condemned the wealthy, property-owning classes. Here's one of my favorites:

> Hear this, you that trample on the needy, and bring ruin to the poor of the land, saying "When will the new moon be over so that we may sell grain; and the sabbath, so that we may offer wheat for sale? We

---

7. Lev 25:8.
8. Deut 15:1.
9. Lev 25:35.
10. Deut 23:19.
11. Lev 19:9.
12. Borg, *Jesus*, 100.

will make the ephah[13] *small and the shekel great, and practice deceit with false balances, buying the poor for silver and the needy for a pair of sandals, and selling the sweepings of the wheat." The Lord has sworn by the pride of Jacob: Surely I will never forget any of their deeds.*[14]

And another:

Alas for those who devise wickedness. . . . They covet fields, and seize them; houses, and take them away; they oppress householder and house, people and their inheritance.[15]

The famous city of Sodom, which God destroys in the book of Genesis, is often thought by conservative Christians to have been targeted because its residents practiced homosexuality. That is blatantly wrong, not least because Ezekiel actually specifies the reason God destroyed Sodom:

This was the guilt of your sister Sodom: she and her daughters had pride, excess of food, and prosperous ease, but did not aid the poor and needy . . . therefore I removed them when I saw it.[16]

One should never make the mistake in thinking that this ire was reserved for foreign powers. In the book of Samuel, Samuel gives the Israelites, who are demanding a king, a famous warning from God about kings. This is presented as the stage at which the Israelites transition from an egalitarian society ruled only by God-appointed judges to a full-fledged, class-based monarchy:

These will be the ways of the king who will reign over you: he will take your sons and appoint them to his chariots and to be his horsemen . . . he will appoint for himself commanders of thousands and commanders of fifties, and some to plow his ground and to reap his harvest, and to make his implements of war and the equipment of his chariots. He will take your daughters to be perfumers and cooks and bakers. He will take the best of your fields and vineyards and olive orchards and give them to his courtiers. He will take one-tenth of your grain and of your vineyards and give it to his officers and his courtiers. . . . He will take one-tenth of your flocks, and you shall

---

13. A unit of measurement for grain. "Making the ephah small and the shekel great" essentially means price gouging.
14. Amos 8:4–7.
15. Mic 2:1–2.
16. Ezek 16:49–50.

be his slaves. And in that day you will cry out because of your king, whom you have chosen for yourselves; but the Lord will not answer you in that day.[17]

The book of Amos begins with condemnations of Israel's enemies, such as Damascus, Tyre, Gaza, and the Ammonites, for their many crimes. Astonishingly, this is followed up immediately by equally harsh condemnations of Israel and Judah, the two kingdoms of God's people:

> *. . . because they sell the righteous for silver, and the needy for a pair of sandals—they who trample the head of the poor into the dust of the earth, and push the afflicted out of the way.*[18]

There are literally dozens of other examples of passages like these, constantly condemning every group of people in the ancient Near Eastern world for their mistreatment of the poor.

An important question to ask is, how seriously was this taken? Were these commandments actually treated as law, or merely as "pious thought," perhaps to be obeyed in spirit but not in practice (which is a contradiction)?

Josephus makes frequent mention of "Sabbath years," so it is extremely likely that they were practiced in some form. How thoroughly is unknown; in modern times, Israeli Jews often get around this practice by temporarily "selling" their land to Gentiles during the Sabbath Year and it is quite possible similar loopholes were employed in ancient times.

More important for our purposes than Sabbath years, however, is the commandment that *"the land shall not be sold in perpetuity, for the land is mine [God's]. With me you are but aliens and tenants"* (Lev 25:23). As alluded to and mentioned before, the significance of this law is that in an agricultural mode of production, land is the most important form of capital.

Knowing this, the purpose of forbidding the growth of a landless class becomes painfully obvious: it was the will of God not only that the poor are "taken care of," or that everyone has enough to eat. It was explicitly that *capital must be distributed evenly so that everyone has access to it.*

Please note that by "capital" I do not mean it in the sense that we often use it in the twenty-first-century, to mean something like "business financing." Leviticus is not telling everyone to become entrepreneurs. Capital is the same as "means of production," and the purpose of distributing it evenly is so that everyone has the capacity to produce for themselves. *Capitalism*

---

17. 1 Sam 8:11–18.
18. Amos 2:6–7.

is a mode of production in which capital / means of production are owned by *capitalists* in the form of private property, and is by definition unequal because *capitalists* need *workers* to work *for* them.

The opposite of capitalism is socialism, when capital or the means of production are owned collectively by society as a whole. In other words, capital is distributed evenly so that everyone has equal access to it, which is exactly what the Levitical law about not selling land in perpetuity means. Imagine a similar law applied to factories, machines, buildings, and land in the twenty-first century; capitalism would simply be unable to function.

It is not inaccurate to say that the Levitical commandment against selling land is anticapitalist; it would be more accurate, however, to say that the commandment is against *class society*, as ancient Israelites did not conceive of capitalism as such. Classes are defined by their relationship to the means of production or capital, and to each other. If capital is distributed equally across society, then by definition there is only one class, which is the same thing as having no classes.

That's all well and good, but what, again, can we say about how seriously this commandment was taken?

The story of Naboth's Vineyard in 1 Kings 21 offers some insight. King Ahab was the seventh king of Israel (Samaria), and his existence is proven by the Assyrian Kurkh Monoliths. He coveted a vineyard neighboring his own, and offered the owner Naboth a much better vineyard in exchange, or the value of Naboth's vineyard in money. Naboth refused, saying, "The Lord forbid that I should give you my ancestral inheritance."

Ahab's foreign wife Jezebel conspires to have Naboth executed, and then tells her husband to seize the vineyard. Ahab does so, and this is presented as a moral event horizon for Ahab; God quickly sends Elijah to condemn Ahab and Jezebel to death for what they have done.

The book of 1 Kings was written several hundred years before the time of Jesus, based on sources that go back even further. It does not definitively tell us how Jews in Jesus's time thought about the commandment to not let land be sold in perpetuity. The story of Naboth's vineyard may or may not have actually happened (Ahab was certainly real and Jezebel was probably real, so Naboth may have been), but its intended meaning is clear: the commandment in Leviticus 25 is serious, and its violation, even by a king, is a grave insult to God.

What all of this tells us is that Judaism has always had embedded within itself a radical current that demands social and economic justice. These sayings exist within the very same texts that condone slavery, genocide, and many other atrocities, and this contradiction must be kept in mind and struggled with. There is no one single understanding of Judaism, nor is there for any other religion. The most important takeaway here is that within Judaism, for a thousand years or more before Jesus was born, there has always been a radical tendency to oppose exploitation and class society.

IN THE BEGINNING

Jesus was a Jew. Everyone knows this, and yet its implications are rarely considered by most Christians. So we begin where the Jews began, with the creation of the universe.

Well, not really. The stories in Genesis, including the two Creation stories (there are two separate ones that are often merged in popular consciousness), are fables, myths, and they are based on even earlier Babylonian stories from tales such as *The Epic of Gilgamesh* and *Enuma Elish*.

Before we delve into the history, allow me one aside into exegesis (that's interpretation of the Bible). It should be useful for understanding the Bible and its relationship to history.

Genesis as we know it today was most likely compiled and composed during the Babylonian exile, when much of the Jewish priestly and scribal caste was held captive within the neo-Babylonian Empire during the sixth century BCE (beginning around the year 597). This helps to explain its suffusion with other ancient Near Eastern mythology, and it also explains the overarching themes of separation and exile (Adam and Eve from the Garden; Jacob and especially Joseph from Canaan). Its authors (who wrote what scholars refer to as the Yahwist and Priestly traditions within the Hebrew Bible) had retrojected their current material reality (exile, Babylon, return from exile to a chaotic homeland) back onto the creation of the universe.

But certainly the traditions in Genesis originate from much earlier than when they were written down and collected into the book we have today. Is there anything of historical relevance in these myths of a tower to heaven, a single original pair of humans, a garden of paradise, a great flood, humans living to be centuries old?

If you are familiar with "Young-Earth Creationism," you may have wondered why exactly this very specific group of conservative Christians dates the earth to be roughly six thousand years old. Why six millennia as opposed to, say, five, or eight?

HISTORICAL CONTEXT

The calculations come from Genesis and its genealogies. In the seventeenth century an Irish bishop named James Ussher used Genesis to calculate the date of creation and came up with the year 4004 BCE. He was not the first or the last to do so; so the question is, why that year? What was happening around that time that left echoes in Jewish creation myths well over three thousand years later?

Things were happening all over the world, of course, but Genesis is helpful also in telling us exactly where to look. "*A garden in Eden, in the east. . . . A river flows out of Eden to water the garden, and from there it divides and becomes four branches . . . Pishon . . . Gihon . . . Tigris . . . Euphrates.*"

This can refer to nowhere else but ancient Mesopotamia, modern Iraq. I will let biblical scholar John Dominic Crossan take it from here: "*Where do we find ourselves when we combine 4000 BCE as time and Mesopotamia as place? . . . We find ourselves amid the climax of the Neolithic Revolution, amid the dawn of civilization, on the mighty plain of Mesopotamia.*"[19]

The Neolithic Revolution marked the transition from hunter-gatherer and horticultural societies to agriculture and "civilization." The parallels are not even subtle; Adam's punishment after being banished from Eden is having to "toil . . . all the days of your life, and you shall eat the plants of the field."[20] Later we are treated to the story of Cain (the farmer symbolizing settled agricultural life) killing Abel (the shepherd symbolizing pastoral nomadic life).[21]

My point here is not that the writers of Genesis knew about the Neolithic Revolution and were consciously creating a fable to mythologize it. They believed their stories were literally true. My point is that fables and myths do not come from a vacuum; I am not an idealist, I am a materialist. There is always a material basis for these types of stories and whether they are literally true or not is irrelevant. What matters is what that material basis is. Keep that in mind as we fly through the history of the Jewish people up to the coming of the Roman Empire.

The Hebrew Bible tells the story of the Jews conquering Israel from the Canaanites at the direction of their God after the exodus from Egypt. There is one major problem with this: there is no archaeological or historical evidence (outside the Bible, of course) that any of it ever happened. Historically, we can be nearly certain that none of it actually happened.

---

19. Crossan, *How to Read the Bible*, 43.
20. Gen 3:17–18.
21. This story also has a Babylonian antecedent in the fable of Dumuzid and Emkindu.

Many Christians and Jews will be uncomfortable or even angry with my saying that, even though it's true. To them I can only shrug and move on. As Reza Aslan said once: "If history says one thing and faith says another, history is correct and it's faith that must be revised."[22]

The Jews did not conquer Canaan and rename it Israel. What actually happened is that the Jews *were* Canaanites, and emerged as the dominant Canaanite tribe around 1000 BCE after uniting the land. This would be around the time of King David, who incidentally is the first biblical figure that we have extrabiblical evidence for.

The Canaanites were a polytheistic ethnolinguistic group who worshiped their own pantheon of deities, the leader of which was El. Many Canaanite tribes were *monolatristic*, meaning they believed in the existence of multiple deities, but only worshiped one. The people who would become the Jews began as worshipers of an idiosyncratic deity named Yahweh, a Canaanite warrior god who entered the pantheon relatively late from Egypt (which may explain the origin of the exodus myth).

When we read the Hebrew Bible (Old Testament) in English, we read God referred to as simply God or the Lord. In Hebrew, however, several different names are used for him, chief among them El and Yahweh. What happened is that as the Yahweh-worshipers conquered or absorbed their neighbors to eventually form the united kingdom of Israel and Judah (more on that in a moment), they began to replace El's position at the head of the pantheon with Yahweh. What began as two separate deities were merged together over centuries until both could be used interchangeably to refer to the same being, who in pre-Judaic times sat at the head of a pantheon of other gods, was depicted in artwork, and even had a wife![23]

There are echoes of this in the Hebrew Bible, but by the time its written form was finalized and compiled during and after the Babylonian exile (probably the most significant historical event in Jewish history up until that point) the Jews had become monotheistic. Again, more on that in a moment.

Around the year 1000 BCE a single Canaanite tribe, who worshiped Yahweh, came to prominence and created the southern kingdom of Judah. Their territory may have extended north into Samaria (Israel), but it would

---

22. I'm paraphrasing, as I cannot remember where I heard him say this (although I am 100 percent positive he did say something very close to it at some point). It may have been in his interview with Cenk Uygur, but I can't stomach watching an hour of Uygur talking anymore to find out.

23. Her name was Asherah, for anyone interested.

be a historical error to view it as some great kingdom spanning all of Palestine. It was most likely a powerful chiefdom led by a chief named David who became powerful enough to call himself king, whatever that term may have meant back then.

David's line endured until at least the ninth century BCE.[24] Over the next several centuries, during and after the time of the united monarchy in the Bible, the cult of Yahweh grew, either through military or cultural imposition, to become dominant throughout both Judah and Samaria. People of both kingdoms began to see themselves as a single people, and this was only heightened after the northern kingdom was conquered and destroyed by the Assyrians in 720.

The southern kingdom, Judah, wisely became a client state of Assyria and so escaped destruction. They prospered until Assyria's defeat at the hands of the neo-Babylonians, who then set their sights on Judah and destroyed it, forcing much of the priestly, scribal, and aristocratic classes to move to Babylon in order to cripple the Jewish peoples' ability to resist.

It was during this period that most of the Hebrew Bible was composed and compiled, and during this period that the Jews truly became the Jews. Monolatrism evolved into monotheism; whereas most ancient peoples adopted the religious customs of their conquerors (or, more accurately, had those customs foisted upon them), the Jews struggled philosophically, politically, and materially to hold onto their identities. This is one of the most central defining characteristics of Judaism—its conception of God is literally based on holding onto a national identity in the face of oppression, subjugation, exploitation, colonization, and imperialism.

BEFORE CHRIST

The identity of the Jewish people arose from contradiction. They worshiped an all-powerful war god, and yet they found themselves again and again conquered and dominated by foreign powers. The Assyrians, the Egyptians, the Babylonians (and many more to come)—if their God was so great, their opponents must have taunted, why were they a nation of conquered, colonized, and oppressed people? This is how the Jews must be understood—as a repeatedly colonized, dominated, and subjugated people.

---

24. The Tel Dan Stele mentions military victories against the northern kingdom of Israel by a Syrian king named Hazael, who was allied with the house of David. Hazael ruled in the late ninth century BCE.

This colonization, domination, and subjugation had a material basis—Palestine (the name the Greeks gave to the region that included Israel and Judah) is situated at the intersection of three continents—Asia, Africa, and Europe. While in better times this made it an important trading center, during worse times this fact meant that the Israelites often found themselves surrounded by competing great empires—Egypt, Assyria, Babylon, Persia, Greece, and many others. If God really promised them the land of Israel, one wonders about God's sense of dramatic irony.

Jewish priests and prophets sought to resolve this contradiction in various ways based on their social class. The priest class (the Jewish ruling class, as it was) sought theological reconciliation between the omnipotence of Yahweh and the plights of his people, and this bleeds into much of the Priestly material in the Torah. P (shorthand for Priestly) is primarily concerned with the formalities and laws of the religious rituals that dominated Jewish life before, during, and after the exile. It originated from the Zadokite (the high priest) tradition and sought to maintain their power and influence by stressing the need to observe these rituals.

The Deuteronomic (D) tradition, meanwhile, originated among the Levites (the lower priests at the time) and reflects their status as a partially subjugated class in its vitriol—the hardships of Yahweh's people were punishments for their unfaithfulness. The contradiction was resolved thusly: Yahweh was still all-powerful, it was merely his will that his people suffered.[25]

Finally, the lower classes were represented by parts of the Prophetic tradition recorded in the Nevi'im (especially the second half, the Latter Prophets). This is especially seen in the concern for social and economic justice found within many of these books, most prominently Isaiah, Amos, and Jeremiah.

The Babylonian Captivity ended in 539 BCE when Cyrus the Great, king of Persia, defeated the Babylonians and allowed the Jewish captives to return home. Cyrus was known for fostering religious tolerance among his subjects, and the Jews were allowed to practice their religion in peace for some time; shortly after returning, the Jews began rebuilding the temple that the Babylonians had destroyed, and the Second Temple period officially began (Jesus lived at the end of this period in Jewish history).

---

25. The Deuteronomic tradition, with its emphasis on covenants, stems from the suzerain-vassal treaties common between client and vassal kings in the ancient Near East, especially between Assyria and Judah. Again, a material basis for an aspect of faith.

It wasn't long before Palestine was conquered again, this time by Alexander the Great. Alexander and his successors spread Greek culture throughout the region and encouraged the growth of the Jewish diaspora throughout the Mediterranean world.

Alexander's empire split and the Israelites found themselves dominated by the Greek Seleucid Empire, who brutally suppressed their Jewish identity to an extent they had not experienced before, attempting genocide through forced conversion and mass slaughter. This period gave rise to the popular Maccabean revolt in 167 BCE, which expelled the Seleucids from Israel and reasserted native control. The Maccabees founded the Hasmonean dynasty and instituted about a century of independence for the Jews, during which they were even recognized by the Roman senate.

It was not to last, unfortunately, as Israel found itself in the middle again of the Roman civil war between Julius Caesar and Pompey and then later Octavius (Augustus) and Marc Antony. By the end, Judea was unified under Herod the Great as a semi-independent Roman client state. Herod ruled for thirty-three years and managed to keep the different regions of Palestine—Judea, Galilee, Idumea, Samaria, and others—united until his death in the year 4 BCE. It is in this year, toward the end of the reign of Herod, that a child was born in Palestine who would alter the course of history for the entire world.

THE TIME OF JESUS

We have already met Herod the Great, and heard what happened in Palestine upon his death. Now we will see this event more broadly.

The Hasmonean Dynasty, which ruled independent Israel (consisting of Judea, Samaria, Galilee, Iturea, Perea, and Idumea) for about a century after ousting the Seleucids, finally ended in 37 BCE, after decades of infighting due to different members siding with different factions during Rome's civil wars in the last century of the era. They were very popular, especially among the Jews, for their role in winning Israel's independence after the brutal oppression of the Seleucids, and the new king, Herod, a half-Jewish half-Idumean, recognized this by taking a Hasmonean woman as his wife.

Israel was officially a "client state" of Rome. What this meant is that it was not a direct province under Roman governorship, but was semi-autonomous and self-governing, so long as the king didn't run afoul of the emperor. Herod played his role well, keeping order and undertaking mass building projects, including renovations to the temple. It is meaningful that revolts only broke out after his death in the year 4 CE.

Herod enforced Rome's will through brutality. While the story of the "Massacre of the Innocents" in Matthew is a nonhistorical fable (there is no historical evidence of anything even remotely like it ever happening, and it is a clear allusion to a similar story about Moses), it is not much more extreme than what we know of Herod's character from Josephus. Toward the end of his life, Herod apparently knew that the populace would celebrate his death: "[Herod's] death would be a thing very desirable, and exceedingly acceptable to them, because during his lifetime they were ready to revolt from him."[26] Josephus then reports that Herod decreed that upon his death, one member of every family was to be executed so that the entire nation would mourn.[27] While this (and a similar order to have a large group of people slaughtered in the hippodrome) order was not carried out, it offers a glimpse into the flagrant disregard for human life that Herod showed.

Perhaps even more than his cruelty and callousness, the Jewish people hated Herod because he had been installed by Rome, had won the throne with Roman soldiers, and paid tribute to Caesar year after year. He was the face of the new foreign, pagan empire that had colonized them.

Matthew's gospel gives the year of Jesus's birth as shortly before the death of Herod, which took place in 4 BCE.[28] If we take this as factual,[29] or even as "in the ballpark," then Jesus was born into a world of massive political unrest. To reiterate, upon Herod's death, as he apparently predicted, revolts broke out all over Palestine. These were quelled, again with the help of Rome, and Herod's kingdom was divided among his three sons and his wife.

---

26. Josephus, *Antiquities*, XVII.6.
27. Josephus, *Antiquities*, XVII.6.
28. The reason that the gospels give Jesus's birth as at least four years "before Christ" is that early medieval scholars working out the chronology of certain events based on the records they had available to them were unable to correctly locate the year of Herod's death, and their misestimations stuck.
29. Ultimately, we have no real reason to take Matthew's account of the year of Jesus's death as factual or not. There is no corroborating or conflicting evidence whatsoever. I assume it is relatively accurate, but at the end of the day, it matters very little what exact year Jesus was born in.

HISTORICAL CONTEXT

Two of these sons are important to know. The first is Archelaus, who inherited Judea, Samaria, and Idumea. The second is Antipas,[30] who took control of Perea and Galilee, where Jesus lived and operated.

Antipas is important because he factors into the Gospel accounts of John the Baptist's execution and was the ruler of the tetrarchy[31] where Jesus lived. Archelaus is important because his rule was short-lived; after being unable to effectively govern, Rome deposed him and instead created the official province of Judea, directly administered by a Roman procurator. The most famous of these was a man named Pontius Pilate.

As the Jewish people entered the Common Era (which, bear in mind, they did not conceive of as such), many of them began to feel that all of their hardships and misfortunes were a part of some divine plan, just as priests and scribes and peasants had thought during previous trials and tribulations. It is around this time that expectations of a messiah began to form in large sections of the population.

Messianic expectation can broadly be understood as a Jewish form of millenarianism. This is the belief that a cataclysmic event will take place in the near future that will radically alter the world. These types of movements are usually found among colonized peoples[32] like the Jews in Roman Palestine. The Jewish Messiah was a "once-and-future-king" archetype who was to be descended from King David and whose role was to drive out all foreign influence and reestablish the united kingdom from the Tanakh. Josephus writes of several rebels and religious leaders around this time who purposefully sought to invoke these messianic expectations in the movements they led, and a couple are also mentioned in Acts.

Millenarian movements, as I alluded to above, do not come into being for no reason. As always, we must examine the material conditions of the society in question to understand why this time and this place was suffused with messianic expectation. We start with, as historical materialism demands, "the production and reproduction of the immediate essentials of life."

We have already discussed the mode of production this society operated under: it was an agrarian slave society. However, under Rome it had

---

30. Herod Antipas, to be exact, who is sometimes referred to simply as "Herod" in the gospels, which creates some confusion. I will only refer to Herod the Great by that mononym; Herod Antipas will always be specified by his given name.

31. One-fourth of a kingdom.

32. Examples include *Ghost Dance* movements; the Xhosa prophet Nongqawuse; Tenskwatawa the Shawnee prophet; the Taiping Rebellion in China; and many others.

the further distinction of being a colonial, colonized agrarian slave society. What this meant is that the ruler, Herod or his son Antipas, had to extract additional wealth from society's producers in order to pay the requisite tributes to Rome. This meant further exploitation of the peasant class and the need for more slaves.

Nobody enjoys being exploited, and forms of exploitation were much more blatant in ancient times than under modern capitalism. It was the mark of a good ruler to be able to measure the amount of wealth they could extract from the peasantry without inciting them to revolt.

That said, there was another element at play that interacted with the exploitation of the Jewish peasantry, and that was the fact that their ruling classes were paying tribute to a foreign, pagan emperor. That term "emperor" must be carefully explained, as well as the man who it referred to.

CAESAR

"Emperor" comes from the Latin word "imperator" which means "commander." During the Republic it was used by numerous political or military leaders and was not an official title. That changed, however, with the first emperor, Caesar Augustus.

Augustus (born Octavian) was the adopted son of Julius Caesar. The two of them were probably the most important players in the series of Roman civil wars that plagued the Mediterranean world for decades during the first century BCE. It all ended, however, at the battle of Actium in 31 BCE, when Octavian finally defeated Mark Antony and Cleopatra and ushered in the *Pax Romana*.

It is difficult to overstate the significance to the Roman world of Octavian's victory at Actium. Suddenly there was peace after literally generations of war spanning the entire empire, and in popular imagination, a single man, Octavian, had brought it. To understand Octavian, you must first understand his adoptive father, Julius.

Julius Caesar had been a much-loved populist leader of Rome during the last years of the Republic. He had won stunning military victories in Europe and commanded the fierce loyalty of his troops. The Roman Senate feared his power and tried to strip him of it, which led to the first civil war within Italy itself. Caesar came out on top, and was proclaimed dictator-for-life.

HISTORICAL CONTEXT

During his reign, Caesar consolidated his own power while instituting sweeping reforms that made him beloved by the masses. He forgave debts, redistributed land, undertook building projects, extended citizenship to people all across the republic, and instituted a new calendar (which is the basis of the one we still use today). He also systematically undermined the power of the Senate by increasing its total membership and giving himself the right to appoint his own loyalists.

Caesar's rule was popular with the plebeians and equestrians (lower aristocrats) and, naturally, quite unpopular among those of senatorial rank (higher aristocrats). His assassination by some influential senators infuriated the masses, including many in the military, and Rome again found itself at war with itself.

Two men sought to avenge Julius Caesar's death, and entered into an uneasy alliance: Octavian, who had been named Caesar's heir; and Mark Antony, a friend of the first Caesar's who had his own ambitions. Together they waged war against the Optimates, chiefly Cassius and Brutus, defeating Caesar's assassins in 42 BCE.

One crucial action they took, spearheaded by Antony, was to declare the late Caesar *divus Julius*, "divine Julius." While a cult of personality had already begun to develop around Caesar before his death, now it spread rapidly through the masses in Rome, encouraged by Antony and Octavian. The pressure was enough for the Senate to officially confirm the divine status of Julius Caesar, which included an official priesthood and temples devoted to him.

The peace did not last long. Antony, who coveted the highest office in Rome, had been surprised by how competent Octavian turned out to be, and how quickly Octavian claimed the loyalty of many of Caesar's former supporters. He hatched a scheme to defeat Octavian in the inevitable third civil war of this period; he formed an alliance and relationship with Cleopatra, the Ptolemaic queen of Egypt, who'd had a biological son, Caesarion, with Julius Caesar.

Octavian now warred with Antony and Cleopatra, and as previously mentioned, defeated them at the Battle of Actium in 31 BCE. What Octavian did next is critical to an understanding of the historical context of Jesus and the gospels.

First, he dealt with the children of Antony and Cleopatra. He executed Marcus Antonius Antyllus, Antony's legal heir and son by one of his former wives. That left three children of Antony and Cleopatra, and Caesarion, the son of Cleopatra and Julius Caesar, Octavian's brother by adoption.

You might expect that Octavian would have killed the children of Cleopatra and Antony, his enemies, and spared the son of his adoptive father, Julius Caesar. In fact, he did the opposite. Alexander Helios, Cleopatra Selene, and Ptolemy Philadelphus were all taken back to Rome alive. Caesarion, the only trueborn son of Julius Caesar, was executed.

Octavian had two reasons for doing this. The first was obviously political: he did not want any competition as the successor to Julius Caesar, who was now a god. While the first Caesar had been divinized after his death, Octavian himself was quickly deified as well, while he still lived and ruled. Part of this was because of his achievements: he had brought peace to Rome. The first-century CE Roman historian Florus wrote:

> *Now that all the races of the west and south were subjugated, and also the races of the north . . . the other nations too, who were not under the rule of the empire, yet felt the greatness of Rome and revered its people as the conqueror of the world. For the Scythians and the Sarmatians sent ambassadors seeking friendship; the Seres too and the Indians . . . the Parthians too, as though they repented of their victory, voluntarily returned the standards which they had won at the time of Crassus' defeat. Thus everywhere throughout the inhabited world there was firmly-established and uninterrupted peace. . . . For all these great achievements he was named Perpetual Imperator and Father of his Country. It was also discussed in the senate whether he should not be called Romulus, because he had established the empire; but the name of Augustus was deemed more holy and venerable, in order that, while he still dwelt upon the earth, he might be given a name and title which raised him to the rank of a deity.*[33]

This was when Octavian became Augustus, which means "one to be worshiped." This was also when "imperator" became more than a simple descriptor. Now it meant something more like "supreme commander" and was only used by the Roman emperors. Rome had officially become an empire.

But Augustus had another reason for executing Caesarion, and it ties into the other reason he had for being deified. Julius Caesar was god. Octavian was Caesar's heir and adoptive son.

---

33. Florus, *Epitome*, XXXIIII.

HISTORICAL CONTEXT

Augustus took another title for himself after becoming Rome's first emperor, and it was a title that by its very nature could belong to only one person.

Augustus became *divi filius*. In English, this title translates to "Son of God."

Sound familiar?

THE END IS NIGH

Jesus lived during the reigns of Augustus and his stepson, Tiberius. While Tiberius apparently shied away from his own cult of personality, he greatly encouraged Augustus's. Coins were minted with Caesar's face on them, and the imperial cults of Julius and Augustus spread throughout the Roman Empire.

This was a problem for many Jews, who by this point in history were firmly monotheistic. It wasn't just the fact that Israel had become a class society against the wishes of Moses and the prophets; it was that they lived under the thumb of a pagan god. Their kings (whether it was Herod the ethnarch or Antipas the tetrarch) paid tribute to a pagan god; the temple, the holiest place in the world, which was supposed to belong only to God, had been opened to Gentiles and was partially under the administration of this pagan god.

It would be a mistake to think of every single Jewish peasant in Palestine as being overburdened with rage and revolutionary furor at this situation. Like all epochs, there was a range of political and religious ideas. Many people went about their daily lives despite the situation in Jerusalem or in Rome. They may have quietly disagreed with the high priest and Sanhedrin's acquiescence to Roman authority, but most of them were not in a position to do anything about it.

There were, of course, exceptions, and they responded to Roman rule in various ways, such as by founding millenarian or other religious revival movements, or taking up arms. John the Baptist, Theudas, The Egyptian, and the Zealots are all examples from the same century as Jesus (the Zealots sparked the war Josephus fought in).

Movements could be millenarian or not, and violent or nonviolent. Theudas's movement, for example, was millenarian but nonviolent; he led a group of people to the banks of the Jordan River and promised to part it like Moses did the Red Sea, which would signal the coming of a new exodus.

The Zealots, on the other hand, were not millenarian but were violent, using guerilla tactics and favoring armed rebellion to expel the Gentile rulers and punish the native collaborators.

It is important to understand that the millenarian movements were not about the "end of the world" as many Christians think of it today. Nobody spoke of the end of the material world; rather, they spoke of the end of the current *age*. The age of foreign domination, of colonization, of inequality and poverty, would end, either by divine intervention or human action or some combination of the two.

This end could be limited to Israel or it could encapsulate all of the nations. While many Jewish revolutionaries and prophets dreamed of political and religious independence for the Jewish people, Jews had for centuries conceived of a radically transformed world that went beyond simple independence.

> *In days to come, the mountain of the Lord's house shall be established as the highest of the mountains, and shall be raised above the hills; all the nations shall stream to it. Many peoples shall come and say, "Come, let us go up to the mountain of the Lord, to the house of the God of Jacob; that he may teach us his ways and that we may walk in his paths." For out of Zion shall go forth instruction, and the word of the Lord from Jerusalem. He shall judge between the nations, and shall arbitrate for many peoples; they shall beat their swords into plowshares, and their spears into pruning hooks; nation shall not lift up sword against nation, neither shall they learn war anymore.*[34]

Note that this peace is not just for the Jews, but for "the nations" and "many peoples." Nor was it limited to the absence of war:

> *A shoot shall come out from the stump of Jesse, and a branch shall grow out of his roots. The spirit of the Lord shall rest on him, the spirit of wisdom and understanding. . . . He shall not judge by what his eyes see, or decide by what his ears hear; but with righteousness he shall judge the poor, and decide with equity for the meek of the earth. . . . The wolf shall live with the lamb, the leopard shall lie down with the kid, the calf and the lion and the fatling together, and a little child shall lead them. The cow and the bear shall graze, their young shall lie down together; and the lion shall eat straw like the ox. The nursing child shall play over the hole of the asp, and the weaned child shall put its hand on the adder's den. They will not hurt or destroy*

---

34. Isa 2:2–4.

HISTORICAL CONTEXT

on all my holy mountain; for the earth will be full of the knowledge of the Lord as the waters cover the sea.[35]

Not only does this transformed world include justice for the poor and the meek, but it's also a totally vegan world where all living things exist together in perfect harmony. A utopian vision, to be sure, but a beautiful one.

So we understand that many Jews in the time of Jesus were dissatisfied, at best, with Roman rule (however remote it may have been). Rome was led by Augustus Caesar, the Son of God, who was himself a god (at least, to the Romans). Why would the almighty God of Israel allow such a thing?

As in similar times throughout their history, Jews struggled with and sought to resolve this contradiction in various ways. Many thought that the current era was coming to an end, for how could it not be? God would not forsake his people; he was always in control.

Because of the way this theology was embedded into the very soul of the Jewish people, the very fact of imperial domination by a foreign god caused them to critically examine themselves. And again, as in similar times before, they looked to the injustices of their world to explain why God was punishing them.

With all of this background, it is now finally time to begin looking at the evidence about Jesus himself. Where did he and his ministry fit into this social world? What was his solution to the contradiction of blasphemous colonization? Was his movement millenarian, or not? Was it violent or nonviolent? Did he claim to be the messiah, or not? Did he claim to be God, or not? Why was he crucified? Why did his movement endure after his death?

Finally and most importantly, what does it all mean for us today?

---

35. Isa 11:1–9.

Chapter 3

PRACTICE

Jesus Christ was a man that traveled through the land, hard working man, and brave. He said to the rich: "Give your goods to the poor!" So they laid Jesus Christ in his grave.

—Woody Guthrie

THE BASIC NARRATIVE

Before diving too deeply into textual analysis of all the little pieces, it's a good idea to step back and consider the whole. The Synoptic Gospels present a relatively simple threefold narrative framework for the life and ministry of Jesus—(1) his miraculous birth in Bethlehem (absent from Mark, of course); (2) his public ministry as an adult in Galilee; and (3) his death in Jerusalem and resurrection three days later. In other words: birth, life, death.

What can we say about this narrative framework? The Passion Narrative of Jesus's death and resurrection will be taken up in a later chapter, while the content of his life and public ministry will form the bulk of this one. That leaves only this small section for the birth/infancy/adolescent narratives.

The story is familiar: Joseph and his betrothed, Mary, who have not consummated their marriage yet, are visited by an angel who tells them

PRACTICE

that Mary will bear the Son of God, even though she is a virgin. They leave their home in Nazareth for Bethlehem, Joseph's ancestral home, so that he can participate in a census. While there they are forced to sleep in a manger where Mary gives birth to Jesus. They are attended by shepherds and visited by three wise men from the east, who followed a miraculous star to the birthplace of the Son of God. Then Herod, having met the wise men and learned of the birth of the Son of God, declares that all male babies born during this time be executed. Joseph and Mary flee to Egypt, and after Herod's death return to their home in Nazareth.

It's a nice story for Christmas, but none of that is how it happens at all. That familiar summary actually contained elements from both Luke's and Matthew's birth narratives, combined into one. Examining the texts side-by-side, however, reveals stark and utterly irreconcilable differences.

The "massacre of the innocents" where Herod decrees that all male babies under the age of two be slaughtered is found only in Matthew, while the census is found only in Luke. Matthew has Joseph and Mary living originally in Bethlehem and moving to Nazareth after the death of Herod and return from Egypt; Luke has them living originally in Nazareth and only going to Bethlehem for the census. Only Luke has the manger; only Matthew has the wise men. Both gospels give genealogies for Jesus, but these genealogies are wildly different. Luke's gospel focuses on Mary, as well as Elizabeth, the mother of John the Baptist; Matthew's gospel focuses on Joseph.

There are other minor discrepancies, but in general what is important to note is that the birth accounts are different in all but four elements: Mary, Joseph, virgin birth, and Bethlehem. So what exactly are we dealing with here?

At first glance, the fact that these narratives appear only in Luke and Matthew may lead one to assume that the birth narrative came from Q. This is extremely unlikely, however; Q was almost certainly a *sayings gospel* like the *Gospel of Thomas*, containing no narratives whatsoever (not counting possible framing devices such as "Jesus said to . . ."). Moreover, the complete lack of textual parallelism other than the four most basic elements makes it very likely that we are dealing with two independent elaborations upon a common tradition.

Of the four elements of this possible tradition—Joseph, Mary, Virgin Birth, Bethlehem—the first two are the simplest to explain. Jesus's parents are named as Joseph and Mary because those were his parents' names.

Mary is mentioned elsewhere, and with the knowledge that Jesus's brothers (especially James the Just) were leaders in the early church it is no stretch to think that their names would have been familiar to many if not most Christians.

Bethlehem is also relatively simple. Our earliest source (Paul) describes Jesus as "Christ"—*messiah*—as does our best non-Christian source, Josephus (recall this was almost certainly in neutral terms, as in Jesus was *called* Christ). In Jewish thought the messiah has to come from Bethlehem[1] because it's the city of King David and the messiah is a Davidic archetype. However, the synoptic account is clear about Jesus coming from Nazareth, which presented a problem for early Christians trying to convince other Jews that Jesus was the Messiah. So Matthew and Luke independently created stories explaining how Jesus could have been born in Bethlehem even though he came from Nazareth.

That leaves only one element, the most important one. The virgin birth is an interesting case, because it seems to defy Jewish convention that is otherwise fairly well-honored in the gospels. There are many examples from the Hebrew bible of miraculous births, however they all involve elderly, infertile women's wombs being opened by God and then being impregnated by their husbands. Mary, on the other hand, is a young virgin impregnated by an act of God.

Much is made of a supposed "prophecy" in the Hebrew Bible from Isaiah 7:14 which reads, "Behold, the young woman is with child and shall bear a son, and shall name him Immanuel." When the Hebrew Bible was translated into the Greek Septuagint (the version the authors of Matthew and Luke knew), the Hebrew *almah* meaning "young woman" was translated into the Greek παρθένος (*parthenos*), which can mean "virgin." However, in the original Hebrew, it has no connotations with virginity, and if you bother to read past Isaiah 7:14 it becomes abundantly clear that the prophecy does not refer to a distant messiah but rather to a situation within the book of Isaiah.

Still, it is unlikely that Matthew and Luke both independently created virgin birth stories based on this mistranslation. Luke shows very little interest in having Jesus directly fulfil prophecies from the Hebrew Bible, and it is highly implausible he would have done so just for that element. More likely is that this tradition was already developing in the late first

---

1. See Mic 5:2.

century and that each gospel author incorporated it into their own account, combining it naturally with the other elements of Jesus's birth.[2]

So what can we make of these elements, historically? The names of Jesus's parents tell us just that, which isn't very helpful (although his mother was probably named after Miriam, the Hasmonean princess executed by Herod the Great [her husband] in 29 BCE. She was well-loved by the Jewish people and her name became very common after her death).

The birth in Bethlehem is more useful. What it tells us is that by the late first century, some early Christians felt the need to invent narratives to bolster Jesus's messianic credentials. Remember, we know that these narratives were invented because none of our earliest sources (Q, Mark, Paul, *Thomas*) make any mention of them. Beyond that, they are suffused with apologetics.

The birth narratives are also not historically feasible. Luke, for example, gets the date of the census under Quirinus wrong, placing it while Herod and Augustus were still alive (in reality it took place long after both were dead). Luke is using the memory of a census from nearly a century earlier as a narrative device to suit his purposes. Likewise Matthew narrates a fictitious story about Herod massacring babies; while we know that Herod was a brutal man, Josephus certainly would have mentioned such a horrific episode as this (as he does with many other of Herod's crimes) had it happened. Matthew is using the relative verisimilitude of the story—Herod was remembered as a violent, brutal ruler—as well as a clear allusion to Pharaoh massacring the Hebrew babies in Exodus, to serve the purpose of drawing allusions between Jesus and Moses (it is no coincidence that he has the Holy Family flee to Egypt until Herod's death).

So the Bethlehem birth is not historical, but it ironically tells us something that is: Jesus was from Nazareth. The fact that neither Matthew nor Luke, with all their interest in retrojecting magnificent origins back onto Jesus's birth, can get around the fact that he was from Nazareth is telling. Nazareth was a tiny, insignificant hamlet in Galilee, and decidedly not where any messiah should be coming from. This tradition's entrance to the literature at this point tells us that when Matthew and Luke were composed, probably between 80 and 90 CE, Christians were struggling against charges that Jesus could not have been the Messiah because he was from Nazareth.

---

2. Even more likely, in my opinion, is the position held by Bart Ehrman, that Luke's gospel originally did not contain a birth narrative. Since this is far beyond the scope of the present work, I will not spend any more time on it, although anyone interested can visit Ehrman's blog for a series of posts about it.

THE CARPENTER'S SON

The final element of the story—the virgin birth—I discount as historical mainly because such a thing is scientifically impossible to the best of our knowledge. However, more to the point, it also enters the canon at a relatively late stage, and Jesus is far from the only ancient figure to be given divine origins by his followers.[3] The virgin birth has no Jewish antecedents, but its usage in Luke, following the barren Elizabeth's conception of John in line with the matriarchs from the Torah, implies that it was meant to show Jesus's miraculous birth as being greater than any previous. An old woman conceiving a child is extremely unlikely, but a virgin conceiving a child is impossible.

There isn't much more to say about the birth narratives. They are beautiful and profoundly meaningful allegories, and serve as overtures for their respective gospels, but for our present purposes we must take them as mostly ahistorical and move on. Barring some wonderful archaeological find, we can say very little about the birth, childhood, and early life of Jesus with any certainty. This may be frustrating, especially to Christians for whom the birth narratives are so central to faith, but it is a reality to be struggled with.[4]

We will turn next to the section of Jesus's life that the gospels are primarily concerned with: his adulthood and public ministry. This will be done primarily by examining the best-attested *pericopes* (units of written material about Jesus) within our sources, as well as paying special attention to *subjects* which appear in multiple plurally-attested pericopes, such as eating or family.

We will *not* be going through each gospel from beginning to end and discussing the historicity of every unit. The first reason for this is simple: this book would be a thousand pages long, or more, and as much as I might like to write a book like that (or read one), few others would be as interested.

The second reason is more important. While the gospels are organized in such a way as to present more or less a continual narrative, at least from Jesus's baptism to his resurrection (and as far as we can tell this structure comes originally from Mark), it is very unlikely that the gospel authors

---

3. Augustus, for example, was conceived by the god Apollo impregnating his mother, according to the Roman historian Suetonius.

4. John Dominic Crossan and Marcus Borg wrote a wonderful book titled *The First Christmas*, arguing that the value of the birth narratives does not depend on their historicity. It is highly recommended. For what it's worth, Christmas is my favorite holiday and time of year and is central to my faith even though I do not believe it literally happened.

intended them to be understood this way, and nearly certain that Jesus's life did not actually happen that way.

In this respect, the gospels are similar to the literary prophets from the Hebrew Bible. These books, such as Amos, Isaiah, Jeremiah, and others, contain the teachings and prophetic exclamations of some of Israel's greatest prophets, but they are not best understood as biographies or chronological tellings of the way in which each prophet prophesied. In her *Introduction to the Bible*, Christine Hayes writes:

> *The prophet's oracles, delivered in various situations over a period of time, were apparently saved and then compiled, perhaps by the prophet himself or by his disciples. We know that prophetic oracles were written down and transmitted in other ancient Near Eastern societies as well (in Assyria, for example). The literary nature of the composition accounts for the lack of chronological order, because the prophets or their disciples would combine prophecies according to principles other than chronology.*[5]

This is exactly what the gospel authors did with the teachings of Jesus. They took things he had said that they knew either from oral tradition or one of their written sources and arranged them in whatever way suited the point they wanted to make. So, for example, the Sermon on the Mount in Matthew is best understood not as an actual sermon that Jesus gave at a specific time in his life, but as a collection of his teachings (as well as possible later teachings put on his lips) that was transmitted orally until finally being written down some time later (in Q) and eventually collected in Matthew and Luke (whose less-redacted version is commonly called the Sermon on the Plain).

To be blunt, knowledge of the exact chronology of Jesus's ministry can probably never be attained. How long did it last? If the synoptic account is taken literally, it would seem to have lasted only about a year. While this is possible, it is unlikely that a movement such as his would have endured had he only been around to build it for a year. It is possible, perhaps even likely, that his public ministry lasted two or even three years, and that he made multiple trips to Jerusalem during this time for Passover (as he does in John's gospel). The gospels tell us that Jesus was "about thirty" at the beginning of his public ministry; this is perhaps true, but ultimately we have no way of knowing.

---

5. Hayes, *Introduction to the Bible*, 250.

While so much uncertainty is, of course, frustrating, once one is able to make peace with it it becomes much easier to focus on the things that actually matter about Jesus: the things he taught and believed.

A VOICE IN THE WILDERNESS

While orthodox Christianity holds that our four canonical gospel accounts—Matthew, Mark, Luke, and John—are essentially four separate eyewitness accounts of the ministry, death, and rebirth of Jesus, this is historically inaccurate. As previously mentioned, they were written at different times, by anonymous authors, decades after the death of Jesus, and three of them (Matthew, Mark, and Luke) show evidence of some interdependence (remember, Mark is original, and Matthew and Luke both used Mark and the lost Q source as the bases for their respective gospels).

By observing how Matthew and Luke used the material they had in common in different ways to tell two distinct versions of the capital-G Gospel, it becomes clear that objective, factual reporting was not the primary interest of the gospel authors. They felt free to move events around, recontextualize certain incidents or sayings, and create framing devices to suit their own purposes.

These literary devices were common for writers in this period. People in the first century were not overly concerned with "facts" the way we in our post-Enlightenment world are. Writing something of your own creation, but placing it on the lips of a famous teacher or spiritual leader, was not considered "libel" even if that's what we might call it today. Authors may have had nefarious motives in doing these types of things, and in some cases their motives may have even directly contradicted the wills of the people they were (mis)quoting, but applying modern standards of journalism to ancient writings is an egregious mistake.

The Synoptic Gospels consist of collections of *pericopes* organized according to the author's purposes. A pericope can be almost anything: a saying, an event, a parable, a command, and they can be as short as a single sentence or paragraphs upon paragraphs long (the birth narratives from the previous section, for example, can be considered pericopes). Each gospel author certainly had their own specific motives for arranging their pericopes in the sequence we find them in today, but that does not necessarily mean that the events described happened in the way that they happen in the gospels.

Given all this, a crucial element of reconstructing the historical Jesus is looking at pericopes individually and considering all the evidence available for each of them. We will begin where Mark, our earliest gospel, began, because it happens to be one of the least controversial pericopes in the entire canon.

Mark, of course, begins with a voice of one crying in the wilderness. "John the baptizer appeared in the wilderness, preaching a baptism of repentance for the forgiveness of sins."[6] A few sentences about John later, "Jesus came from Nazareth of Galilee and was baptized by John in the Jordan."[7]

Now, this pericope (Jesus being baptized by John) only has one single attestation, in Mark (Matthew's and Luke's versions are dependent on Mark, so they don't count). However, by analyzing the texts to see how each successive author treated this pericope, we can argue strongly in favor of its historicity.

Recall the "criterion of embarrassment" I mentioned earlier. This is when a detail in the gospels would have embarrassed the early Christian communities, so they would have no reason to invent it and it is most likely historical. Since the gospels intended to exalt Jesus, it's unlikely they would have fabricated a story where another figure had authority over Jesus. Therefore the baptism is most likely historical. This is a general argument, however an examination of the text reveals obvious attempts to correct this embarrassment with each successive gospel.

In Mark, John foretells the coming of "he who is mightier than I,"[8] and then Jesus simply comes and is baptized by John. The gospel moves on. Clearly Mark, the earliest of the canonical gospel authors, isn't *too* bothered by it. A simple statement from John that Jesus is mightier will suffice.

Next comes Matthew, who has John protest Jesus's request for baptism, quite sycophantically: "I need to be baptized by you, and do you come to me?"[9] Jesus reassures John and convinces him to go through with it in order to "fulfill all righteousness." In this exchange, clearly Jesus is dominant.

In Luke, the baptism is rushed and diminished in favor of no less than God's exaltation of Jesus. After listing some of John's commands to his would-be followers, Luke simply remarks: "Now when all the people

6. Mark 1:4.
7. Mark 1:9.
8. Mark 1:7.
9. Matt 3:14.

who were baptized, and when Jesus also had been baptized and was praying . . . the Holy Spirit descended upon him in bodily form, as a dove."[10] The baptism is still present, but is mentioned only in passing.

Finally the process is completed in the Fourth Gospel, which makes no mention of the baptism of Jesus by John whatsoever. John the gospel writer, writing nearly a century after Jesus's death, is either too embarrassed by the idea of Jesus being baptized by John (the Baptist) to include it, or simply does not know the tradition (which may be an even stronger argument in its favor, ironically).

So the baptism of Jesus by John is one of the most historically certain events in the life of Jesus that we know of. But we can go further and posit that it is likely that Jesus was a full-fledged disciple of John for a longer period of time than is implied by the gospels.

We also know about John from Josephus, who records (in corroboration with the Synoptics) that John was executed by Antipas. Josephus and the gospel accounts differ, however, as to the content of John's teaching and the reason for his execution. This discrepancy is an interesting case study in the way the class interests of an author color their view (speaking of Josephus here).

We know from Acts 18 and 19 as well as the following account from Josephus that John the Baptist still had followers and supporters decades after his death. This may help to explain why Josephus's account of John differs from the synoptic account. When recording a military defeat that Antipas suffered, he writes:

> Now some of the Jews thought that the destruction of Herod's army came from God, and was a very just punishment for what he did against John called the Baptist. For Herod had him killed, although he was a good man and had urged the Jews to exert themselves to virtue, both as to justice toward one another and reverence towards God, and having done so join together in washing. For immersion in water, it was clear to him, could not be used for the forgiveness of sins, but as a sanctification of the body, and only if the soul was already thoroughly purified by right actions. And when others massed about him, for they were very greatly moved by his words, Herod, who feared that such strong influence over the people might carry to a revolt—for they seemed ready to do any thing he should advise—believed it much better to move now than later have it raise a rebellion and engage him in actions he would regret. And so John,

---

10. Luke 3:21–22.

> *out of Herod's suspiciousness, was sent in chains to Machaerus, the fort previously mentioned, and there put to death; but it was the opinion of the Jews that out of retribution for John God willed the destruction of the army so as to afflict Herod.*[11]

This is a stark contrast with the synoptic account, which unequivocally states that John's baptism was indeed for "the forgiveness of sins." Also compare the banal John of Josephus's imagination who only baptized those "already thoroughly purified by right actions" and whose only crime was apparently being too popular and telling the Jews to be virtuous (???) with the John of the gospels who, like Jesus, preached the coming kingdom of God, polemicized against the Pharisees and Sadducees, and ordered the Jews to share freely of their belongings with the needy.

It may be tempting to assume that the gospel authors purposefully made John more like Jesus, but this does not fit with their agenda of downplaying John's influence in Jesus's life. Their version of events also makes much more sense than Josephus's, as a ruler like Antipas would be much more likely to execute a charismatic prophet who speaks truth to power and proclaims a coming kingdom than a benevolent hippie who just tells people to be nice to each other.

Finally, Josephus's class interests must be considered. He was an aristocratic Jewish historian living in Rome, and at least one purpose of his writings about the Jewish people was to defend the Jews to his gentile audience. It makes perfect sense that he would sanitize John the Baptist into a figure the Roman upper classes would find palatable, especially considering that John's popularity continued after his death. Indeed this latter fact is important to bear in mind for our reconstruction of Jesus, as Acts has the following story:

> *Now there came to Ephesus a Jew named Apollos, a native of Alexandria. . . . He had been instructed in the Way of the Lord; and he spoke with burning enthusiasm and taught accurately the things concerning Jesus, though he knew only the baptism of John. He began to speak boldly in the synagogue; but when Priscilla and Aquila heard him, they took him aside and explained the Way of God to him more accurately.*[12]

Apollos, a Hellenic Jew who was likely an admirer or even follower of John the Baptist (the very next event in the narrative of Acts narrates

---

11. *Antiquities*, XVIII.5.
12. Acts 18:25–26.

Paul's meeting with other followers of John), is described as well-versed in Scriptures and having received instruction in the Way of the Lord (ὁδὸν τοῦ κυρίου), but knowing only "the baptism of John." Famous missionary couple Priscilla and Aquila apparently took him under their wings and he became a prominent and powerful evangelist for Christ.

What this (along with the succeeding narrative in Acts 19) tells us is that there were enough similarities between the messages of Jesus and John for John's followers to have been easy to convert to Christianity decades after the deaths of both men. Indeed someone like Apollos, who "knew only the baptism of John," was nevertheless also knowledgeable enough to teach "the Way of the Lord."

Given all this evidence, a reasonably safe conclusion is that the messages of Jesus and John were similar in at least some ways. Because of the evolving tradition of downplaying John's influence in Jesus's life, it is likely that Jesus was a disciple of John before starting his own ministry. By reading between the lines of Josephus, we can surmise that John's message involved repentance, the remittance of sins, moral and ethical teachings, and opposition to the governing authorities. This is all corroborated by the synoptic account.

We will return to John in a while; for now we will focus on Mark's next and most important major theme: the kingdom of God.

YOUR KINGDOM COME

If you were somehow able to re-read the Synoptic Gospels for the first time with absolutely zero context about Christianity or even Judaism, what would you take away from them? Stripped of two millennia's worth of Christian apologetics and Jewish evolution, what would you make of this Jesus character?

You would almost certainly come away with the sense that Jesus was overly concerned with something called the kingdom of God.[13] Indeed, the single unanimous opinion about the historical Jesus among scholars is that his teachings and movement revolved around his concept of the kingdom

---

13. Matthew uses the phrase "kingdom of Heaven" instead. This is almost certainly a circumlocution for "kingdom of God" in keeping with the Jewish aversion to using the word "God" in some contexts. It is a metonymy, similar to how we often say "the White House" when we mean "the president."

of God.[14] Mark certainly wants you to think this. That is why the first words Jesus utters in his gospel (and thus in the entire existing synoptic tradition) are, "The time is fulfilled, and the kingdom of God has come near; repent, and believe in the good news" (Mark 1:15).

Such scholarly consensus, alas, only goes so far, for most of these scholars would vehemently disagree with each other about what that kingdom actually entails. There are two major fronts in this debate—the *content* of the kingdom, and its *form*.

Where to begin? The content refers to what the kingdom actually looks like, what it means to live within it. The form refers to the method of the kingdom's arrival; how will it be brought about? Analyzing both is not an easy task, for these two issues—content and form—form a powerful dialectic that makes it difficult to explain them sequentially, for they are actually quite intertwined.

We will do our best, however, to start with *form*. We will begin, as we did with the previous section, where Mark began, with the very first words our earliest gospel puts on the lips of Jesus: *"The time is fulfilled, and the kingdom of God has come near [ἤγγικεν]; repent, and believe in the good news."*

It is no accident that these are the first words uttered by Jesus in the gospel tradition. Mark is signaling the ultimate thesis of Jesus's entire mission: that the kingdom of God is near.

But what does it mean, exactly, that the kingdom has come or is coming near? Is it like an object in space and time, approaching physically? Is it near in time but beyond space? Is it within reach? Does it exist in another sense, beyond time and space, attainable somehow?

This is a question of eschatology (*eschaton* means "final" or "end" in Greek). Recall the discussion of millenarian movements from earlier; the kingdom of God is best understood as a millenarian movement calling for the end of the current *age*. The coming of the kingdom of God meant the end of the kingdoms of the earth (including Rome, which thought of itself as a "kingdom" at the time; the term "empire" is only how later historians characterize it). Importantly, as previously mentioned, this does not mean the end of the physical world but the end of the current state of being.

---

14. New Testament scholar John Reumann once wrote, in *Jesus in the Church's Gospels*: "Ask any hundred New Testament scholars around the world, Protestant, Catholic, or non-Christian, what the central message of Jesus was, and the vast majority of them—perhaps every single expert—would agree that his message centered in the kingdom of God."

The traditional view of scholars is that Jesus was an apocalyptic prophet, teaching that the kingdom of God was on its way and would forcibly displace the current world order. There are two main arguments for this: one is that John the Baptist was also allegedly an apocalyptic prophet, as were the earliest Christians after Jesus (although their eschatology was centered in the Parousia of Jesus). If Jesus's forerunner was apocalyptic, and his successors were apocalyptic, it follows that he probably was as well. We will examine this argument shortly.

The second main argument in favor of an apocalyptic Jesus is that numerous sayings attributed to him in the gospels seem to be apocalyptic in nature, especially sayings concerning the "Son of Man."

Opponents of this theory generally argue for a "realized eschatology,"[15] meaning that the kingdom of God is somehow present in the world already and that it is the duty of believers to participate in it. In this understanding, the kingdom is not some external, displacing force that will overthrow the current world order, but a participatory program of liberation that can somehow overthrow the current world order from within.

So which is accurate? Which understanding is closer to what Jesus taught? We must examine the available evidence.

The verb ἤγγικεν (*ingiken* in modern pronunciation, ἐγγίζω or *engizo* for the infinitive), meaning "to come near" or "to approach," occurs fourteen times in the Greek perfect tense, which according to J. Schlosser has connotations of "extreme *closeness*, immediate imminence—even a *presence*,"[16] and according to Werner H. Kelber "[refers] to an event which happened in the past but continues to be of relevance for the present."[17] Be that as it may, a close analysis requires taking inventory of every pericope about the coming of the kingdom and analyzing what they have to say about it. For this argument I am reliant especially on the works of John Dominic Crossan and Helmut Koester.[18]

John the Baptist, as previously mentioned, is generally thought to have been an apocalyptic preacher, baptizing sinners in preparation of the imminent arrival of the kingdom of God. Interestingly (and tellingly), this notion comes mostly from Matthew, the most apocalyptic of the gospel

---

15. This term was coined by C. H. Dodd.
16. Quoted on BibleHub, https://biblehub.com/greek/1448.htm.
17. *Kingdom in Mark: A New Place and a New Time*; quoted by J. D. Crossan, *Historical Jesus*, 345.
18. See Crossan, *Historical Jesus*; Koester, *Introduction to the New Testament*.

authors, so there is a distinct possibility that John was not as apocalyptic as he has long been thought to be.

But for the sake of simplicity, let us assume that John was explicitly apocalyptic; that is, he preached that God was about to dramatically intervene and claim lordship over a united, independent Israel. Since Jesus began as a disciple of John, it is safe to assume that at least initially, Jesus accepted John's eschatology.

But what do we find when we collect the earliest and best-attested kingdom sayings throughout the gospels? I have used those identified by John Dominic Crossan in his book *The Historical Jesus: The Life of A Mediterranean Jewish Peasant*, with slight modification.[19] These are the sayings most likely to be authentic words of Jesus because, as Crossan puts it, they are the ones "where at least two independent sources claim the Kingdom expression."[20] I have only included these sayings which Crossan, relying heavily on Koester and others, identifies as appearing within the first (earliest) stratum of material, plus a single saying from Mark that also appears in the independent *Shepherd of Hermas*.

These sayings are, by name/general summary: *Kingdom and Children*,[21] *The Mustard Seed*,[22] *Blessed the Poor*,[23] *When and Where*,[24] *Two as One*,[25] *The Lord's Prayer*,[26] *Greater than John*,[27] *The Planted Weeds*,[28] *The Pearl*,[29] *The Leaven*,[30] *The Treasure*,[31] and *Kingdom and Riches*.[32]

These sayings can be divided into four categories regarding their eschatological implications: ambiguous, neutral, apocalyptic, and

---

19. I've added a single saying, *Kingdom and Riches*, and only focused on the sources Paul, Q, Mark, Special L, Special M, and *Thomas*, with a couple of exceptions.
20. Crossan, *Historical Jesus*, 459.
21. Appears in *Thomas*, Mark, Special M, John.
22. *Thomas*, Mark, and possibly Q.
23. *Thomas*, Q, James.
24. *Thomas*, Q, Mark, Special L.
25. *Thomas*, Paul.
26. Q, *Didache*.
27. *Thomas*, Q.
28. *Thomas*, Special M.
29. *Thomas*, Special M.
30. *Thomas*, Q.
31. *Thomas*, Special M.
32. Mark, Shepherd of Hermas.

anti-apocalyptic (favoring a "realized eschatology"), plus a unique fifth category that deserves special attention. By my judgment:

Kingdom and Children, *Kingdom and Riches*, and *Blessed the Poor* are neutral;

Only *The Treasure* is ambiguous (this is one of Jesus's most confusing parables, and the disparate versions in Matthew and *Thomas* don't help);

Lord's Prayer and *The Planted Weeds* are unambiguously apocalyptic;

Mustard Seed, *Two as One*, *Greater than John*, *The Pearl*, and *The Leaven* are anti-apocalyptic;

And finally *When and Where* is apocalyptic in some forms, anti-apocalyptic in others. This requires careful explanation and hinges on the term "Son of Man."

Before we get to that, let us deal with the other two explicitly apocalyptic sayings, *Lord's Prayer* and *The Planted Weeds*.

The Lord's Prayer comes to us in three versions; one in Matthew, one in Luke, and a third in the *Didache* that is extremely similar to Matthew.

If we accept the two-source answer to the Synoptic Problem, which I along with most scholars generally do, it seems clear that Luke's shorter version of the prayer, which lacks any apocalyptic connotations whatsoever, is earliest. Generally, shorter forms of sayings are likely to be earlier; writers are much more likely to add than subtract. Matthew, as I've noted, is by far the most apocalyptic of the Synoptic Gospels, and it makes sense for him to have added a plea for the kingdom to hurry up when he was adapting from Q. The inverse theory, that Luke used Matthew as a source, claims that Luke took the second petition away because Luke had an anti-apocalyptic bias. This may sound convincing unless you know that (a) Matthew had already intensified the apocalyptic aspects of Mark, and (b) Luke preserves other apocalyptic sayings intact.

So the apocalyptic reference in the *Lord's Prayer* is a probable interpolation from Matthew that later found its way into the *Didache*.[33] It certainly does not go back to the historical Jesus, although it is a useful encapsulation of some of his teachings (daily bread, a kingdom on earth, forgiveness of debt; we will return to it later).

---

33. This does not mean the *Didache* was directly dependent on Matthew. By the time the *Didache* was finalized the Matthean version of the Lord's Prayer could very well have become commonplace among various Christian communities; it may not have originated with Matthew at all. Matthew may have added petitions he already knew to the original version from Q, or the version of the prayer in the *Didache* may have been a later layer of the document.

The Planted Weeds, found in *Thomas* 57 and Matthew 13:24–30, speaks of weeds being separated from the good wheat and burned at the time of harvest. It is an interesting addition to *Thomas*, which is generally anti-apocalyptic. In any case, Matthew shows his hand a few passages later, when he has Jesus clumsily interpret this parable to his disciples: "The one who sows is the Son of Man; the field is the world, and the good seed are the children of the kingdom; the weeds are the children of the evil one, and the enemy who sowed them is the devil; the harvest is the end of the age, and the reapers are angels" (Matt 13:37–39).

This reminds one of Augustine's and Origen's allegorical interpretation of the Good Samaritan, in which literally every element of that story is a stand-in for something else (the inn, for example, is the church). This way of reading parables has been criticized by everyone from John Calvin to C. H. Dodd. The idea that Jesus himself would interpret his own parable (which defeats the purpose of a parable) in such a heavy-handed way is, quite frankly, absurd, and so Matthew's usage if not the saying itself must fall under heavy suspicion.

And now we turn to *Where and When*, the most telling of the early kingdom sayings. In *Thomas* 3, 51, and 113 and Luke 17:20–21 it is explicitly anti-apocalyptic. *Thomas* repeats three times that the kingdom is already present, but people do not see it, and Luke beautifully says that the kingdom is "among you" (εντός υμῶν). Matthew, as he is wont to do, is just as assertive in the other direction.

The difference here is that while these sayings are all similar, there is actually an important distinction between the apocalyptic and non-apocalyptic ones. *Only in the non-apocalyptic sayings does the word "kingdom" actually appear.* The apocalyptic versions of the passage all refer not to the kingdom, but to the "Son of Man."

The term "Son of Man," which is attributed to Jesus throughout the gospels, originates in the apocalyptic visions in the book of Daniel. In the seventh chapter, Daniel is having a prophetic dream of four beasts, one like a lion, one like a bear, one like a leopard, and one that is "different from all the beasts that preceded it" (7:7). The beasts are superseded by the coming of "one like a son of man" (RSV 7:13) or "one like a human being" (NRSV), who will rule "all peoples [and] nations," and whose dominion "is an everlasting dominion . . . and his kingship is one that shall never be destroyed" (7:14).

That difference in translation reflects the NRSV's attempt at modernizing the language of the Bible as well as removing gendered language; the literal translation is "son of man" but the meaning is "human being."

Now the four feral beasts are identified with great empires of the ancient world; their identities are disputed, but there is a general consensus that the first is the Chaldean Empire (which had destroyed Solomon's temple and caused the Babylonian exile). The Medes, the Persians, the Macedonians, the Seleucids, and the Romans are all seen as possible identifiers for subsequent beasts; generally I find it most believable that the fourth beast represents Alexander's Macedonains *as well as* the Seleucids. Consider the explanation of the fourth beast starting at Daniel 7:19, which mentions that "out of this kingdom ten kings shall arise, and another shall arise after them" (7:24); this "another" probably represents the Seleucid Empire.

This part of Daniel originates in the mid-second century BCE, when the Jewish people were partially subjugated by Antiochus IV Epiphanes, the ruler of the Seleucid Empire (which eventually led to the Maccabean Revolt). Antiochus outlawed the Sabbath and circumcision, and forced Jews to make pagan sacrifices in the temple. Consider the very next passage: *"This one shall be different from the former ones. . . . He shall speak words against the Most High, shall wear out the holy ones of the Most High, and shall attempt to change the sacred seasons and the law; and they shall be given into his power for a time, two times, and half a time"* (7:24–25). This last part refers to the amount of time the Maccabean revolt lasted (about three and a half years, see 1–2 Macc).

So Daniel 7 and beyond is essentially Maccabean propaganda claiming that with Maccabean control of the Jewish homeland, the "kingdom of God" or the final climactic kingdom was fulfilled. Son of man is *not* a title in any sense yet. What eventually happened is that when Jesus began preaching a very different vision of the kingdom of God (because Maccabean rule obviously didn't last long and Israel found itself under foreign rule once again), Daniel had to be reinterpreted as a prophecy of things yet to come to pass. So by the first century CE, it is conceivable that "Son of Man" *could have* been used legitimately as a title for the one who would bring God's climactic, apocalyptic kingdom.

The question remains, however, whether Jesus himself actually used this title in that way. It is used mainly in the Synoptic Gospels, and only by Jesus to refer to himself. It also appears once in Acts (written by Luke) and twice in Revelation, when quoting Daniel 7, but never in the letters of Paul.

PRACTICE

Geza Vermes shows definitively[34] in *Jesus the Jew* (p. 168) that in Galilean Aramaic (the language Jesus spoke), "son of man" (*bar nash*) was used not infrequently as a circumlocution for "I," always referring to the speaker. It carried no eschatological or even theological connotations of its own, and no example of it being used as a title (outside the New Testament) exists (Daniel, by the way, was written in Aramaic).

Vermes then charts every single Son of Man saying in the synoptic tradition, and the results are striking. If you discount sayings that only appear in Matthew *or* Luke, but not both, only two sayings directly reference Daniel, and both are originally from Mark. Five reference Daniel indirectly (1 from Mark, 4 from Q), and a whopping sixteen have *no apocalyptic connotations whatsoever* (11 from Mark, 5 from Q).

This, along with other evidence based on philology and history, leads Vermes to conclude:

> *There is no evidence whatever, either inside or outside the Gospels, to imply, let alone demonstrate, that "the son of man" was used as a title. There is, in addition, no valid argument to prove that any of the Gospel passages directly or indirectly referring to Daniel 7:13 may be traced back to Jesus. The only possible, indeed probable, genuine utterances are sayings independent of Daniel 7 in which, in accordance with Aramaic usage, the speaker refers to himself as the son of man out of awe, reserve, or humility. It is this neutral speech-form that the apocalyptically-minded Galilean disciples of Jesus appear to have "eschatologized" by means of a midrash based on Daniel 7:13.*[35]

Because we cannot reliably take the apocalyptic "son of man" sayings as authentic sayings of the historical Jesus, the apocalyptic elements of the "*Where and When*" kingdom sayings must be seen as later eisegesis by the early Christians. Thus, when we look at all of the early and best-attested kingdom sayings, the ones most likely to go back to the historical Jesus, we see that they overwhelmingly support a non-apocalyptic eschatology.

We have thus far focused on negative evidence; now we will briefly consider several more positive clues. I want to be emphatic that these positive examples are secondary; the preponderance of non-apocalyptic kingdom sayings and the weakness of the "son of man" sayings are the primary arguments. These serve only to confirm and corroborate.

---

34. Vermes, *Jesus the Jew*, 168.
35. Vermes, *Jesus the Jew*, 185–86.

Essentially, seriousness must be given to the question of *why* Jesus would have gone against not only his own mentor John, but the common Jewish belief in a coming divine intervention.

There is one very simple, by no means new explanation that makes perfect sense. If Jesus went to John to become baptized, then he accepted (initially) John's message that the kingdom would be coming soon. He may have even believed John to be the messiah; certainly there was no shortage of messianic claimants in that time and that place.

But then Herod killed John, as we know from the Synoptics and Josephus. In the gospels this happens after Jesus's ministry is already underway, but that is only explicit in Matthew and Luke. In Mark, the narrative of John's execution is told in flashback form and the time frame is unclear. Actually, given that in Mark Herod thinks "John, whom I beheaded, has been raised," of Jesus, it actually implies that it was not until after the death of John that Jesus's movement became known, which given the short span of Jesus's ministry, suggests that it did not even begin until after John's death.

Matthew and Luke copy Mark's story, but before it they include the episode of John sending messengers from prison to ask Jesus if he truly is the Messiah. There are several problems with assigning historical status to this event; first, it conflicts with what we just saw, that Jesus's ministry most likely began in earnest after John's death; two, Jesus almost certainly did not claim the title of Messiah for himself (see Vermes, *Jesus the Jew*) and if he did it would certainly have been long after John's death; three, Jesus's reply about the blind receiving sight, etc., is a clear reference to Isaiah 35, which suggests that this is exegesis, not history. It also precedes the genuine saying of Jesus praising John the Baptist, so this event is most likely a literary creation meant to avoid, again, the "embarrassment" of Jesus's exaltation of John.

So I say it is a fair assumption that Jesus accepted John's program, was baptized into his movement, and after John's arrest may have stepped up into an unofficial leadership position while they waited. John was in prison; surely the kingdom would be arriving any day now.

Then Herod executed John, and God did *nothing*. There was no climax, no ceremony, and no consummation (it is useful to note that there was no idea of a messianic Parousia in Judaism until after the death of Jesus).

So what was a zealous Jew who longed for God's justice to do? He could have continued John's program verbatim, taking over as the figurehead and likely meeting the same fate as John eventually. But what reason was there to believe that God would intervene the second time, if he hadn't the first?

Or, as an alternative, his theology could be refined and his vision of the kingdom updated. Perhaps it was God who was doing the waiting, and the mission of humans to actively build the kingdom on earth.

So Jesus began his Kingdom Movement, which was intended as a large-scale paradigm shift of Jewish Messianic thought, accounting for the experience of John's execution. Instead of waiting for the kingdom, Jesus taught that the kingdom was already present. Like the mustard seed it is small but grows to overtake all others; like leaven it is mixed all throughout the dough to make it expand; like the pearl it is available immediately to anyone willing to part with their wealth; the lowest members of the kingdom now are greater even than John; you can enter the kingdom by abandoning hierarchy and class distinction in your life.

Further evidence is given by something Jesus's enemies accused him of. He was apparently charged with being "a glutton and a drunkard" (Matthew 11:19 = Luke 7:34). This is explicitly contrasted with John's celibate asceticism: "For John came neither eating nor drinking, and they say 'He has a demon'; [Jesus] came eating and drinking, and they say, 'Look, a glutton and a drunkard.'"

Is there more to this than the hypocrisy of Jesus's critics? Was there some higher significance to Jesus's meal practice?

Consider also Luke 10:7–8, Jesus's instructions to the seventy disciples. He says to them, "Remain in the same house, eating and drinking whatever they provide. . . . Whenever you enter a town and its people welcome you, eat what is set before you."

This saying has a parallel in *Thomas* 14, where the meaning is more explicit: "If you fast, you will bring sin upon yourselves. . . . When you go into any region and walk about in the countryside, when people take you in, eat what they serve you."

Thomas combines this with the saying from Matthew 15:11 ("it is not what goes into a person's mouth that defiles him"), which is interesting because it means that saying 14 contains both a saying that appears only in Matthew, and one that appears only in Luke.

Be that as it may, it is clear that the gospel authors have recontextualized all of these sayings. Jesus's practice of dining with the people he healed and preached to had a special significance, which will be discussed later, but based on this evidence it is also relevant here.

The idea of a fasting prophet would have been familiar to most Jews. The Essene community practiced an extreme form of asceticism, and numerous prophets of the Hebrew Bible, from Moses on Sinai to Elijah in the Nevi'im, fasted, sometimes for as long as forty days. No such paradigm of a "gluttonous" prophet, however, exists, and it is emblematic of Jesus's subversive tendencies and the seeming shift in theology and eschatology he preached.

Put simply, John fasted because the world was about to end. Jesus instructed his followers to do the opposite in order to sound the opposite message: the world is not ending; the kingdom of God is here, now, and of this world.

The debate over the apocalypticism of Jesus will rage on for a long time to come, but in my opinion the majority consensus[36] in favor of apocalypticism can be mostly chalked up to most scholars simply taking it for granted because that's what they've been taught, as well as a general lack of a convincing case for what this present kingdom of God actually looked like. Building this case is our next task.

FOOD AND DRINK

I want to stay with that last passage we discussed, about Jesus being a glutton and a drunkard. The issue of Jesus's meal practice comes up several times in the synoptic tradition, so it deserves attention. The following will inventory every relevant pericope from the synoptic tradition that involves eating, meals, table fellowship, etc.

Eating with Sinners

Mark 2:15–17 (paralleled in Matthew 9 and Luke 5):

> *As he reclined at dinner in Levi's house, many tax collectors and sinners were also sitting with Jesus and his disciples. . . . When [the Pharisees] saw that he was eating with sinners and tax collectors, they said to his disciples, "Why does he eat with tax collectors and sinners?" When Jesus heard this, he said to them, "Those who are*

---

36. It is a majority but by no means overwhelming consensus. Scholars who have dissented include Dodd, Crossan, Koester, Marcus Borg, Geza Vermes, Stephen Patterson, and others.

well have no need of a physician, but those who are sick; I have come to call not the righteous but sinners."

A brief aside about the Pharisees, who in this and many other incidents are portrayed as having criticized, defamed, and mocked Jesus and his followers. The Pharisees were a popular and devout sect within Second Temple Judaism that had been important political leaders during the Hasmonean era, but by the time of Herod and his sons were diminished in authority. Still, Josephus reports that they were very popular and well-respected among the population at large. They were known for having their own unique interpretations of Mosaic law, which they took very seriously (although did not try to force onto others).

Pericopes about Jesus being criticized and attacked by the Pharisees are unlikely to be historical. Josephus reports that they numbered in the thousands around the time of Jesus, but these were most likely concentrated in Judea and especially Jerusalem. There were very few (if any) Pharisees wandering the villages and rural areas in backwater Galilee during the time of Jesus. What is much more likely is that in the decades after Jesus's death, as Christianity grew into a competing sect within Judaism, the early Christians came into conflict with the Pharisees over adherence to Mosaic law. The gospel authors retrojected the Pharisees onto authentic stories about Jesus as well as created their own to serve as polemics against their rivals.

All that being said, the fact that the Pharisees were criticizing the early Christians on their eating practice is still informative, especially if we can determine that early Christian meal practice was in direct continuance with that of Jesus himself. So let us continue.

The Bridegroom

Mark 2:18–20 (paralleled in Matthew 9 and Luke 5):

> *Now John's disciples and the Pharisees were fasting; and people came and said to him, "Why do John's disciples and the disciples of the Pharisees fast, but your disciples do not fast?" Jesus said to them, "The wedding guests cannot fast while the bridegroom is with them, can they? As long as they have the bridegroom with them, they cannot fast. The days will come when the bridegroom is taken away from them, and then they will fast on that day."*

There are two things to note about this saying. The first is that the saying about the bridegroom has an alternative version in *Thomas* that lacks the comparison with John. Mark has combined two separate historical facts into a single pericope: the question of why Jesus and his disciples did not fast even though his mentor John had; and a saying about the bridegroom. It is a natural synthesis to make and the fact that Mark combined them does not detract from the historical value of either piece of data.

The saying about the bridegroom illustrates that the kingdom is cause for celebration and joy, not mourning and sorrow. The implication that Jesus is the bridegroom soon to be taken is a post-Easter exegesis on a saying that probably referred originally to the kingdom and its members, including but not limited to Jesus.

The second important thing to note is that a different saying, found in the Q tradition (aforementioned in the previous section, Luke 7 and Matthew 11) corroborates the contrast between John's asceticism and Jesus's supposed gluttony. The extant versions of this saying are suffused with apocalypticism, but for our present purposes it is that original core, the divergence between John's asceticism and Jesus's gluttony, that is important. This points not only to a break from John's practice, but also to food or meal as an important part of Jesus's. This becomes explicit with the next saying.

Feeding the Multitudes

Mark 6:40–44 and parallels:

> *So they sat down in groups of hundreds and of fifties. Taking the five loaves and the two fish, he looked up to heaven, and blessed and broke the loaves, and gave them to his disciples to set before the people; and he divided the two fish among them all. And all ate and were filled; and they took up twelve baskets full of broken pieces and of the fish. Those who had eaten the loaves numbered five thousand men.*

These narratives, found in multiple versions in all four canonical gospels, are generally counted as "nature miracles" when indexing pericopes, but since they relate to food we will briefly consider them. In both stories Jesus and his disciples are flocked by thousands of excited onlookers, but there is not enough food to feed all of them. Jesus performs a miracle by multiplying loaves of bread and fish so that thousands of people are fed. The stories are obviously mythological and recall Elisha performing a similar miracle in 2 Kings. Furthermore, John Dominic Crossan has argued persuasively that these nature miracles were created primarily to answer problems of apostolic succession in the post-Easter decades when Christianity was still forming. They are allegorical, not historical. However, the emphasis on Jesus and his followers feeding a multitude fits snugly within this complex of historical sayings/deeds about food and also evidences that food was an important aspect of early Christianity.

The Lord's Supper

Mark 14:22–25 and parallels; 1 Corinthians 11:23–26:

> *While they were eating, he took a loaf of bread, and after blessing it he broke it, gave it to them, and said, "Take; this is my body." Then he took a cup, and after giving thanks he gave it to them, and all of them drank from it. He said to them, "This is my blood of the covenant, which is poured out for many. Truly I tell you, I will never again drink of the fruit of the vine until that day when I drink it new in the kingdom of God."*

The Lord's Supper or Last Supper is ostensibly the basis for what is probably the most important ritual in Christianity, the Eucharist. The historicity of the actual event will be taken up later as it is a part of the Passion Narrative, but for now we note that the earliest mention of this saying/tradition actually comes from Paul, writing in the 50s CE before any of the gospels were written. We will reserve judgement on the origin of the Eucharist for later; the important thing now is that the very earliest layer of our tradition contains decisive evidence of a Christian ritual centered on meal, implying that meal/food was in some way important to the Christian mission. That word "mission" is very deliberately chosen, as we will see in the next and most important pericope.

The Mission

This pericope is attested in Mark 6:6–13, Q,[37] and the *Gospel of Thomas*, so I will focus on it at some length. Matthew's (10:5–10) and Luke's (10:1–9)

---

37. This can be demonstrated by how Matthew and Luke both treat it. Matthew, using Mark and Q, harmonizes both versions into a single account. Luke, on the other hand, uses both, and so this pericope appears twice in different versions in his gospel.

versions are both given here, as they are the ones that explicitly mention food and they are different from each other in important ways. (Luke has two versions, by the way; this is the latter version.)

> Matthew: *[Jesus sent the Twelve] out with the following instructions:* "Go nowhere among the Gentiles, and enter no town of the Samaritans, but go rather to the lost sheep of the house of Israel. As you go, proclaim the good news, 'The kingdom of heaven has come near [ἤγγικεν, *ingiken*].' Cure the sick, raise the dead, cleanse the lepers, cast out demons. You received without payment, give without payment. Take no gold, or silver, or copper in your belts, no bag for your journey, or two tunics, or sandals, or a staff; for *laborers deserve their food.*" (emphasis added)

> Luke: *After this the Lord appointed seventy others and sent them on ahead of him in pairs to every town and place where he himself intended to go. He said to them,* "The harvest is plentiful, but the laborers are few. . . . Carry no purse, no bag, no sandals; and greet no one on the road. Whatever house you enter, first say, 'Peace to this house!' and if anyone is there who shares in peace, your peace will rest on that person; but if not, it will return to you. Remain in the same house, eating and drinking whatever they provide, for *the laborer deserves to be paid.* Do not move about from house to house. Whenever you enter a town and its people welcome you, eat what is set before you; *cure the sick who are there, and say to them, 'The kingdom of God has come near to you* [ἤγγικεν, *ingiken*].'"

Mark's version of this pericope does not mention eating except for the directive for the disciples to take "no bread" with them (which still implies that they should get their food from the people they minister to). Matthew and Luke each add their own reference to eating, and the differences are meaningful. Matthew references food as payment for the labor of preaching and healing, which Paul also states is a teaching of Jesus, quite independently of the synoptic tradition.[38] Luke, meanwhile, has Jesus specifically command the seventy eat and drink in the houses that host them, but uses the word μισθοῦ (wages) instead of Matthew's τροφῆς (*trophos*, food). These are both important because Luke's version makes explicit what is implicit in Mark and Matthew, namely that eating with their hosts is not simply a by-product of this mission but an integral part of it; while Matthew's version, combined with Paul's reference to the same teaching, gives us a saying of Jesus that we can be relatively certain is authentic.

38. 1 Cor 9:4, 14.

PRACTICE

This pericope is one of the best-attested in the entire canon. Elements of it appear independently in Paul, Q, *Thomas*, Mark, and the *Didache*. From this, we shall form a hypothesis, which will then be tested against further evidence.

My hypothesis is that Jesus's ministry revolved around an ongoing mission (or multiple finite missions) in which his disciples (not simply the Twelve) would travel the countryside, providing the healing and remittance of sins characteristic of Jesus's practice in exchange for food and shelter from the people they served. If this is the case, I expect to see three pieces of corroborating evidence: (1) Additional sayings within the synoptic account that point in this direction; (2) Evidence that the first few generations of Christians practiced something like this; and (3) A cultural-anthropological explanation for this practice that fits with the rest of what we know of Jesus's mission.

I see five additional sayings appearing in the synoptic account that may indirectly point to such a mission. (Pericopes that point more directly will be taken up momentarily as they relate to early post-Easter Christianity.) These are (a) *Kingdom and Children*,[39] (b) *Another Exorcist*,[40] (c) *The Great Banquet*,[41] (d) *Whoever Receives You*,[42] and (e) *One Who Serves*.[43]

A) This saying about the kingdom belonging to children (Mark & parallels) has a disparate version in *Thomas* that relates to eating, specifically breastfeeding. Jesus says that those who enter the kingdom are like infants being nursed. The kingdom involves physical as well as spiritual nourishment, as well as a dependency; just as an infant depends on its mother for nourishment, members of the kingdom depend on those they minister to for nourishment.

B) In this tale, the disciples tell Jesus that another person, unknown to them, was having success as an exorcist in Jesus's name. Jesus rebukes them for trying to stop him, declaring that anyone not against them is for them. Jesus continues that those who give his disciples "a cup of water to drink because you bear [my name]" will be rewarded. Exorcism will be taken up later, but what we take from this now is (i) that

---

39. Mark 10:14–15 and par.; *Thomas* 22.
40. Mark 9:38–41 and par.
41. Matthew 22:1–14 = Luke 14:15–24; *Thomas* 64.
42. Mark 9:37.
43. Luke 22:27 and par.

the healing/exorcising mission was open to everyone; and (ii) that providing for the physical nourishment of these exorcists (water in this case) was a part of that mission.

C) The parable of the great feast (or wedding feast) has been redacted to hell by both Matthew and Luke from its original form in Q. Matthew's version is a disaster; Luke's is better, but the simplest and probable closest to the original can be found in saying 64 of *Thomas*. This saying will be analyzed in greater detail later; for now we simply note the emphasis on the kingdom as a great feast partaken of by the poor, outcast, the disabled, etc., and excluding the wealthy and powerful. It is the servants of the master (seen as the members of the kingdom) who go out to bring the poor into this great feast.

D) This and the next saying form a tangled web of sayings that have been cut-and-pasted together by the gospel authors. Mark has *Whoever Receives You* combined with a saying about *whoever wants to be first must be last and servant of all*; Jesus then picks up a small child and says that whoever welcomes a child in his name is welcoming him, and whoever welcomes him welcomes "the one who sent me" (meaning God; this part is a later addition). Matthew and Luke copy this, but Matthew adds the line about giving a cup of cold water, this time to the child, that we saw earlier in *Another Exorcist* in Mark.

E) Luke's version of this saying is given primacy even though it originates from Mark because Luke's version is likely much closer to the original.[44] Mark and Matthew add a Son of Man saying clearly indicative of post-Easter Parousia-expectation. The original parable about the kingdom of God relates to food because it is about sitting around a table, and it corroborates the theme found in the prior saying of service as crucial to one's place in the kingdom. Jesus clearly states that he is like a servant at a dinner table, and that the greatest in the kingdom are also like servants.

I see this emphasis on service, corroborated by multiple sayings, as providing the theoretical groundwork for this evangelizing mission of the Twelve, the seventy, the seventy-two, or most likely anyone who wished to participate in the kingdom. These sayings may help to strengthen my hypothesis, but alone they are inconclusive. Next we see if we can find

---

44. See, e.g., Vermes, *Authentic Gospel of Jesus*, 240–41.

evidence of such a mission from the earliest Christian communities. I do not presume, by the way, that such a mission *must have* continued after Jesus's death, but if we can find evidence that it did, it makes the argument in favor of such a mission being historical much stronger.

I see two places in our evidence of early Christianity that such a practice did, in fact, continue, and even remained central to the work of the earliest Christians for some time after Easter. These places are in the letters of Paul, and the *Didache*.

The ninth chapter of 1 Corinthians is devoted to "the rights of an apostle" and of course this does not refer only to the Twelve, who Paul often mentions as such. He is protesting that he, like all the other apostles as well as Jesus's brothers and Peter, has "the right to food and drink" on his evangelizing missions to the Greek cities he and Barnabas traveled to. He asks sarcastically if it is only he and Barnabas, alone among Christian missionaries, who "have no right to refrain from working for a living." "If we have sown spiritual good among you, is it too much if we reap your material benefits? . . . The Lord commanded that those who proclaim the gospel should get their living by the gospel."

We will say more about Paul's interpretation of this commandment shortly, but here we have corroboration that Jesus really did command that his itinerant followers should be compensated with food and that this mission continued (in possibly altered form) after his death.

Second, we have the *Didache*, an early manual for Christian practice (dating to around the turn of the second century or earlier) that is most likely literarily independent of the Synoptic Gospels.[45] The *Didache* echoes some precepts found in Matthew (although it actually may predate Matthew, see Tomson) about fasting and prayer, and clearly presumes that the Christian movement (still in its infancy) is based on a system of itinerant preachers/prophets/teachers being paid in food:

> *Let every apostle that comes to you be received as the Lord. . . . And when the apostle goes away, let him take nothing but bread until he lodges; but if he ask money, he is a false prophet. (Didache* 11)

> *But let every one that comes in the name of the Lord be received. . . . But if he wills to abide with you, being an artisan, let him work and eat; but if he has no trade, according to your understanding see to it that, as a Christian, he shall not live with you idle. (Didache* 12)

---

45. See the work of van de Sandt, especially *Matthew and the Didache* and *Matthew, James, and Didache*. See also Tomson, "Didache, Matthew, and Barnabas."

This is clear evidence of a mission *like* what I have hypothesized Jesus commanded his followers do. It shows two major developments. First and foremost is that the healing/exorcism aspect is gone, or at least hidden. Again, this topic will be touched upon more later, but for now I infer that a mission focused on charismatic healing and exorcism would have found success among peasants in rural areas and small villages, but would have been embarrassing for metropolitan, Hellenized Jews and Gentile god-worshipers in cities. By the time the *Didache* was in use, the mission had changed or was changing from rural to urban.

Second, there is apparently the presumption that these wandering prophets/missionaries will work to earn their keep. The *Didache* repeats what was likely an original commandment of Jesus: that the itinerants should not remain with their hosts for more than a day or two. It develops this further, however, by commanding that if they do end up staying longer they should have some sort of trade with which to support themselves.

This is a significant development because it has a parallel in one of the pseudepigraphical Pauline epistles, 2 Thessalonians. There one of Paul's literary descendants, writing in his name, also warns against idleness and recommends that food not be shared with those who will not work to support themselves. This is directed at settled members of the Christian community and there is no mention of itinerant missionaries, one of many indications that this letter is a later creation. But it does echo what the real Paul mentioned earlier in 1 Corinthians, which is that he refused his "right" to be fed and housed by the people he ministered to while on his own itinerant mission.

What we see here is a clear development of a mission from the time of Jesus to the end of the first century when it faded. The original mission Jesus gave to his followers involved the sending out, in pairs, of believers to heal and proclaim the coming of the kingdom to all who would receive them. In return, those receivers would feed and house the wanderers.

After Jesus's death the mission began to shift. As we have seen earlier, his earliest followers, including his brother James and the Twelve, settled in Jerusalem and formed a commune. But the itinerant mission continued and Paul even partook in it, although it shifted from a rural mission focused on healing and exorcism to an urban mission focused on proselytizing. By the end of the century it was waning as Christianity became apostolic and grounded in settled church assemblies in Greek cities. The itinerant preachers were settling down or retiring and the younger generation wasn't taking their places.

The evidence is strong enough to say confidently that something like this process did take place. There was some kind of mission involving itinerant preachers/healers and a system by which they would be fed and housed by the people they ministered to. Some version of this mission continued after Jesus's death, because it was never meant to be a single, limited undertaking. Our final task is to put it in a larger social context: what was the significance of this mission? What do cultural anthropology and historical materialism tell us about what this could have meant?

We're still focusing on food now. The term used in anthropology to discuss matters of table and food is *commensality*, and Jesus's meal practice has rightfully been called *open* commensality or even *radical* commensality. He not only sat down to eat with undesirables such as sinners and tax collectors, but instructed his followers to do so as well and taught that doing so was how one entered the kingdom. Why?

The seminal work on the subject is Gillian Feeley-Harnik's *The Lord's Table: The Meaning of Food in Early Judaism and Christianity*. "Meals . . . symbolize proper behavior among social groups in relation to one another and in relation to God. Who may eat what with whom is a direct expression of social, political, and religious relations," she writes.[46] Commensality can also be a conscious practice: "In establishing precisely who eats what with whom, commensality is one of the most powerful ways of defining and differentiating social groups. It may be used to represent kinship or connubium. It may also be used to establish a community of interests, marking close relationship, among those who are neither kin nor affines."

Food and commensality had long held a place of primary religious significance for the ancient Israelites.[47] Feasts marked the most important events from Israel's history, most obviously the Passover feast to celebrate Yahweh's deliverance of his people from slavery in Egypt. These feasts were ritual meals on a national scale, and through them the nation as a whole came together one day a year in commensality to celebrate their shared heritage.

The kosher dietary laws are also of paramount importance for properly adhering to Mosaic law and especially were so during the time of Jesus. While the commands to abstain from pork, shellfish, and certain other

46. Feeley-Harnik, *Lord's Table*, 2.
47. Feeley-Harnik, *Lord's Table*; see also Smith, *Lectures*.

animal foods probably did not have a single common origin, in practice they served again to bind the nation together. They were things that Israelites did not do, a way of forming a national identity, that became religionized over the course of centuries.

And again, historical materialism reminds us that *the determining factor in history is, in the final instance, the production and reproduction of the immediate essentials of life.* Food and water are the most immediate of the immediate essentials of life, especially in a preindustrial society that is at the mercy of famines, pestilences, and other food shortages. One does not need to be a trained anthropologist to have an implicit understanding that access to food, and the ways in which individuals and groups organize the procuration and consumption of food, is of supreme importance to who we are as individuals and as members of a group.

W. Robertson Smith put it excellently in the late nineteenth century when he wrote, "*The very act of eating and drinking with a man was a symbol and a confirmation of fellowship and mutual social obligations. . . . Those who sit at meal together are united for all social effects; those who do not eat together are aliens to one another, without fellowship in religion and without reciprocal social duties.*"[48]

What is happening here is that Jesus and his followers were modeling the way social relations were ordered in the kingdom of God, which was both a present reality and a future state of all the world. The kingdom was comprised, quite literally, of the marginalized and dispossessed uniting in shared material resources.

It is time now to move on to the other half of *the Mission*. The missionaries were paid in food not for telling their hosts about Jesus, but for sharing another important resource, this one spiritual instead of material. The other key to this mission was free healing, grounded in the charismatic healing and exorcism abilities of Jesus himself.

HEALING THE SICK

A directive of Jesus's followers who undertook *the Mission* was to heal the sick while proclaiming the kingdom of God. This includes exorcism; healing and exorcism are two sides of the same coin and so will be considered together. Indeed, Jesus makes explicit the connection between exorcism and the kingdom in a saying from Q:

48. Smith, *Lectures*, 269.

PRACTICE

> *But if it is by the finger* [Matt: Spirit] *of God that I cast out demons, then the kingdom of God has come to you* [ἔφθασεν]. (Luke 11:20; Matt 12:22)

First note the different word for where the kingdom is than in *the Mission*. *Ephthasen*, which is used here, connotes something arriving forcefully or overwhelmingly while *ingiken*, which is the Markan formulation (Mark 1:15), implies physical nearness. Q has this saying next to a saying also included in Mark (the Beelzebul controversy) and so Matthew and Luke both embed it there as they harmonize Mark's and Q's versions of this saying. However, the usage of the distinct verb *ephthasen* (which does not appear anywhere else in the synoptic tradition) instead of *ingiken* argues in favor of the saying's authenticity, as it cannot have resulted from a single mistranslation or creation by a Greek author, but rather by two different Greek authors translating the same saying or similar sayings with different words.

Healing and exorcism are among the more challenging topics for modern Western people to grapple with when learning about the historical Jesus. Healing we understand, but generally only in the context of modern medical science. We understand faith healing, but except for the more conservative, traditional, or mystical (if I'm feeling generous) believers among us, faith healing is seen as harmless but ineffective at best and a sinister charade that causes worse sickness and even death at worst. Exorcisms are simply alien and foreign, relics of an earlier time period when people believed demons interacted with the material world.

In understanding the form and function of Jesus's healing and exorcism miracles, we need to jettison all of these preconceived notions. An anthropological-materialist understanding of healing and exorcism puts these miracles into a context that helps immensely with the present reconstruction.

First, a few textual notes. Healing/exorcism miracles are attested numerously throughout the synoptic tradition as well as John, but no individual pericopes have more than double-attestation from our earliest sources. There is also a tendency as the material is reused through the gospel trajectory to de-emphasize certain unsavory aspects of Jesus's healing miracles.

Twice in Mark, Jesus heals using spittle and incantations. This ritualistic form of healing could easily have been construed as magic, which was forbidden in Judaism. In Mark 7 Jesus is said to have healed a deaf-mute by spitting on his hands, touching the man's tongue and ears, and speaking the Aramaic word *Ephphatha*, which means "be opened." Later in Mark 8, Jesus heals a blind man by spitting on his hands and touching the man's eyes; this time the healing ritual takes two tries to work.

This was all obviously embarrassing for some early Christians, as evidenced by how neither Matthew nor Luke copy either of these stories. (Interestingly, John also contains a story of Jesus using his spit to heal a blind man—mixing it with dirt to form mud. John suffuses it with mysticism and spiritual exegesis.) These aspects—spit, mud, speaking a word of power meant to address or entreat a higher being, the possibility of a ritual not working the first time—are all very common motifs within the context of magic and occult practices in the Mediterranean world.[49] This image of Jesus would not have sat well with most Jews and even some Gentiles, so it had to be erased.

Again we take our *criterion of embarrassment* to say that historically, Jesus probably did incorporate some magical and/or ritual practices into his healing process. I will make a positive value judgment on that claim; while Christianity has of course long had an antagonistic relationship with practitioners of magic, systems of magic, the occult, and indigenous healing are often religious expressions of resistance to oppression.

In 1979, Arthur Kleinman and Lilias H. Sung published a landmark study called *Why Do Indigenous Practitioners Successfully Heal?* They observed the shamanistic healing practices of hundreds of cases from Taiwan and China, both places that have been colonized by foreign powers in the twentieth century. The patients of these shamans reported staggering success rates (upwards of 80%), although the authors note: "It is likely our results are skewed toward more positive evaluations of healing, since it is reasonable to assume that the clients who refused to be interviewed were more likely to harbour negative evaluations of their treatment" (12).

This and related studies help us both to wrap our heads around what actually took place when Jesus and his followers healed the sick as well as contextualize it for our larger reconstruction. We will take these one at a time.

Kleinman and Sung note an astonishing fact about those patients that reported successful treatment: 40 percent of them reported either minimal, no, or even *negative* symptomatic improvement. Put another way, "In some cases symptomatic change was the chief determinant, while in others behavioral change was most important. For example, cases no. 4 and no. 6 experienced no symptomatic change, but derived psychological benefits

---

49. Luck, *Arcana Mundi*.

and probably also social benefits (e.g. they got out of the house, away from family problems, socialized with friends, enjoyed the exciting atmosphere, etc.) from their treatment."[50]

What we are seeing here is the difference, long understood in anthropology but less so in popular consciousness, between *healing illness* and *curing disease*. Disease and illness are two different things. Disease refers to the pathology that interferes with biological systems; illness refers to the psycho-social experience of having that disease. While Kleinman notes that Western medicine focuses almost exclusively on disease, throughout most of human history and in most indigenous medical systems, disease and illness are often treated together, made indistinguishable. That is how a patient can report being successfully "healed" by a shaman even though the physical symptoms of the disease have actually worsened.

This is what we are dealing with in the healing and exorcisms of Jesus and his followers. "The treatment of disease plays a small role in the care of these disorders," Kleinman writes. "The indigenous practitioner usually (but not always) is exceptionally well poised to maximize psychosocial and cultural treatment of the *illness*" (24, my emphasis). Although he does not use the terms "illness" and "disease" in this way, Georg Luck in his book on magic in the Greco-Roman world argues that the healing ministry in question "had to include physical, mental, and spiritual health."[51]

Modern Western Christians tend to think of Jesus's miraculous healings as demonstrations of his divinity, his uniqueness, his special connection with God. While there isn't *nothing* to this reading, it is superficial and misses the fact that Jesus lived in a world where healing by magic, exorcism, or faith was not considered all that out of the ordinary. Even in the Hebrew Bible, the pagan Egyptians sorcerers are able to engage in a magical duel with Moses, going tit-for-tat with him for some time before being defeated by Yahweh. This was a culture and a world that did not have a scientific outlook on the natural world; to them, magic simply existed and was as real as the wind or the water.

Since we *do* have the benefit of natural science, I am willing to positively assert that magic is not real and that the efficacy of faith or folk healing, such as it is, at curing disease is attributable to the therapeutic nature of the process of *healing illness*, as well as the placebo effect. Jesus's healings probably had great success in treating psychological or psychophysiological

---

50. Kleinman and Sung, "Why Do Indigenous Practitioners," 13.
51. Luck, *Arcana Mundi*, 180.

diseases, but that does not mean that he was always successful. As Kleinman noted, those with negative evaluations of their healing experience rarely report back to the healer, and we have no way to do follow-up examinations on any of Jesus's patients.

We can admit these things while still holding onto the fact that Jesus was almost certainly an exceptionally gifted folk healer and exorcist. He was not a charlatan peddling snake oil; he and all of the people who lived in his world sincerely believed in what they were doing, and it often had positive results. But why was it so central to the larger mission Jesus was undertaking? Why did the act of healing or expelling evil spirits bring forth the kingdom of God?

The answer is found within the context of where people in Jesus's time thought disease came from. In practice, Jesus's healing and exorcisms were a direct challenge to the real, earthly authorities of his people.

WHO CAN FORGIVE SINS BUT GOD ALONE?

Recall Jesus's mentor John and what Josephus wrote about him. I will reproduce an abridged version of the key section for convenience:

> [John called the Baptist] was a good man and had urged the Jews to exert themselves to virtue, both as to justice toward one another and reverence towards God, and having done so join together in washing. For immersion in water, it was clear to him, could not be used for the forgiveness of sins, but as a sanctification of the body, and only if the soul was already thoroughly purified by right actions.

Josephus's unprompted assurance that "it was clear to [John]" that baptism "could not be used for the forgiveness of sins" all but confirms that the purpose of baptism indeed was for the forgiveness of sins. The synoptic account states this directly, and also portrays Jesus as being criticized for this exact transgression.

The case in point is found at the beginning of chapter 2 of Mark (and then in Matthew 9 and Luke 5). It also appears in John 5, independently of the synoptic account in Mark.

In this story, a paralytic is brought to Jesus in Capernaum, but the crowd around Jesus is so large that the paralytic's friends have to lower him to Jesus from the roof. Jesus immediately proclaims that the man's sins are forgiven, which enrages some scribes because it is blasphemy. Jesus taunts them and heals the man's paralysis as proof that he (the Son of Man) has the authority to forgive sins.

There are two important things to note about this. The first is that the paralytic is brought to Jesus for healing, not explicitly for the forgiveness of sins. Jesus proclaims his sins forgiven without being asked. This displays the implicit connection between sickness and sin (in the minds of the Jews of this time) that has already been discussed. The second is that while Mark and Matthew have Jesus's opponents as simply "scribes"[52] Luke has "scribes and Pharisees." This evolving element (see the section above about the Pharisees) tells us that this controversy about the forgiving of sins continued into the Apostolic Age, and thus was likely an original element of *the Mission*.

The forgiveness of sins by John, Jesus, or their followers was not simply an issue of blasphemy, or of hypocrisy on the parts of his critics. Forget about two thousand years' worth of Christian exegesis about sin for a moment. Sin in Second Temple Judaism was not always as dramatic as Christianity has made it out to be, nor was there any concept of "original sin." Jews, and especially first-century Jews, had very different ideas about sin and redemption. Any violation of Mosaic law as spelled out in the Torah could be considered a sin. The Law section of the Tanakh covered nearly every aspect of Jewish life, from business to economics to interpersonal relations and, perhaps most importantly, ritual purity. Central to the concept of ritual purity was the temple in Jerusalem (the second temple of Jesus's time).

"Sin" in this case is not the same thing as "ritually impure." The torah is very clear that there are certain situations where devout Jews are expected to become ritually impure, such as when burying their dead or during menstruation. In these situations, however, there are specific prescriptions, usually involving washing rituals or a sacrifice at the temple, for becoming pure again.

"Sin" or "sinner" then refers to something greater. Sinners were people in a constant or near-constant state of transgression of Mosaic law. This included Gentiles, but more importantly it referred to Jews who did not (or could not) properly follow torah as mediated by the central authority of the temple. There are many types of people this could refer to, and what they all have in common is class.

---

52. John has "the Jews," which is a whole other can of worms.

The destitute would not be able to afford the temple sacrifices that ritual purity required, or even the trip to Jerusalem if they lived further away. Prostitutes, beggars, thieves, day laborers, and slaves could all find themselves trapped in a cycle of "sin" from which it would be very difficult to escape, both in the practical sense of standing with the temple and the more intangible sense of the judging stares of their neighbors. Those who could not wash themselves; those who had to eat whatever food was available to them, kosher or not, or starve; those who slept on the streets near dead bodies for lack of a home; those who took any kind of work they could find; those who were disabled and unable to provide for themselves or perform the rituals; these people made up the "sinners" who were systemically unable to access the forgiving intercession of the temple.

A brief aside: when I call these people sinners, I mean it in the sense that Jews in John's and Jesus's world would have meant it. The more privileged of this world (like Josephus) looked at the destitute and saw sinners, thanks in no small part to a heaping of Deuteronomic theology which taught that sin is the cause of misery, thus if you are miserable you must have sinned. But this was by no means a universal view in Second Temple Judaism; indeed many Wisdom writings such as Job and Ecclesiastes offer differing conceptions of sin, misery, and punishment. Deuteronomic theodicy, however, was central to the ideology underpinning temple authority.

So how do we understand John's and Jesus's "forgiveness of sins" in light of all this? Again, Josephus's special pleading that the people John baptized had "already thoroughly purified by right actions" (including proper purity rituals) tells us that the opposite was most likely true. A special washing ritual for respectable members of society already in full communion with the temple is not a movement that attracts devoted followers or makes kings tremble in fear.

More likely John's baptism served exactly the function Josephus tells us it didn't: it was a ritual for the forgiveness of sins targeted at those people who, for whatever reason, could not, did not, or would not escape their "sins" through approved means. Washing was a common element in Near Eastern purification rituals (including within the temple), and John's presence on the Jordan River, where the Israelites first crossed into the promised land in the book of Joshua, symbolized the baptized person's reentry into the promised land of God's kingdom.

The forgiveness of sins and surrounding controversy was not about Jesus placing himself on equal footing with God; that is a post-Easter development of the early church. Jesus and his disciples healing the sick and forgiving sins was a challenge to the monopoly the temple claimed on access to the cleansing, purifying, and forgiving services of God. It was only blasphemy if you identified God with the temple, which of course most or many Jews of the time did. Was Jesus perhaps trying to proclaim a different message? Was he saying something about the temple itself?

THE RULERS OF THE WHOLE WORLD

The temple was many things to the Jewish people. The original temple (Solomon's temple), which had been destroyed by the Babylonians in the early sixth century BCE, features prominently in many narratives in the Hebrew Bible. It was the center of ritual, sacrificial, and cultic practices for the ancient Israelites, and most of the Mosaic covenant presumes it as such. Therefore its rebuilding was one of the first projects undertaken after the Babylonian captivity.

This rebuilding took centuries and was still being worked on until shortly before the time of Jesus. Josephus narrates a speech by Herod; after lamenting that the Second temple had not yet regained the former greatness of Solomon's temple, he said to his people:

> *Our fathers, when they returned from Babylon, built this temple to God . . . so much did that first temple which Solomon built exceed this temple. [Do not] let anyone condemn our fathers for their negligence . . . for it was not their fault that the temple was no higher . . . but since I am now, by God's will, your governor . . . and I am at amity with and well regarded by the Romans, who, if I may so say, are the rulers of the whole world, I will do my endeavor to correct that imperfection.*[53]

Note the immediate contradiction. The Romans are the "rulers of the world," yet Herod is the governor "by God's will." The implication is that Rome is the ruler of the world by God's will. This probably was not troubling to people like Josephus or Herod, who were comprador collaborators with Rome and owed their great privilege and status to Rome. But how would a poor devout Jew have heard these words? How would a zealous and proud Jew have heard these words?

---

53. *Antiquities*, XV.11.

So again the fundamental contradiction in the soul of ancient Judaism crops up. And again the Jews of Israel sought to resolve it in different ways.

The Sadducees, representative of the aristocratic and priestly classes, simply ignored the contradiction and stressed strict torah adherence. They had an individualized interpretation of world events, disbelieving in fate and stressing that everyone's station in life was as a result of their own choices and that by one's own actions one could prosper. They also didn't believe in an afterlife. Unsurprisingly (and hilariously, in my opinion), Josephus reports in *Antiquities* XII.10 that they "are unable to persuade anyone but the rich."

The Pharisees, on the other hand, did believe in eternal reward or punishment based on adherence to the law, which included an "Oral Torah" consisting of interpretations and additions to the original Mosaic Covenant. They were, as previously mentioned, very popular and their school of thought evolved into Rabbinic Judaism. They resolved this contradiction into a non-antagonistic one; the Romans may have instituted Herod, and they may have had to pay a temple tax to Rome, but they could still practice their religion and look forward to the general resurrection in the future if they lived virtuously.

The Essenes lived ascetically, removing themselves from the corrupt temple system to form a new, separate religious order in their small communities. They lived pastorally and communally, holding all property in common, and did not marry because they expected the end of the world to come soon. They kept to the law, but eschewed animal sacrifice. They also appear to have conducted their own washing or water-immersion rituals.

The Zealots, according to Josephus, held similar ethical and cosmological views as the Pharisees, "but they have an inviolable attachment to liberty, and say that God is to be their only Ruler and Lord." This led them to periodic armed revolt, culminating in the Jewish-Roman War of 66 and the destruction of the second temple. They assassinated many of the temple priests and, during the war, seized control of the temple itself, attempting to form a revolutionary government and priesthood, selecting a new high priest by drawing lots.

These were the four main currents of Jewish thought during the Second Temple period, especially just before, during, and after the life of Jesus. Note that all of their defining characteristics centered on temple worship and the relationship of the temple to Rome. That is what is at stake with this question, and how it ties back to the forgiveness of sins and the realization of the kingdom of God in the act of healing/forgiving. The task at hand is to discern how Jesus (and his mentor, John) fit in to this fourfold typology, if at all.

We can safely discard the Sadducees as being of any influence on Jesus's thought whatsoever. Jesus definitely did not ignore the contradiction between Roman rule and God's authority; if he had, they wouldn't have crucified him. The crucifixion happens, at least in the synoptic narrative, as a result of Jesus staging a sort of demonstration or action in the temple itself; while we will take up the details of the cleansing of the temple in the chapter on the passion as a whole, for now we take it as historical only that Jesus's ministry in some way was opposed to the temple.

My proposition is that John and Jesus represent a unique fifth response to the contradiction of the temple's corruption, which shares characteristics with the Pharisees, Essenes, and Zealots, but is also different from each of them. Furthermore, that Jesus, after John's execution, developed this fifth response even further beyond John (see the earlier section about apocalypticism).

Like the Pharisees, Jesus delivered many oral teachings meant to supplement (not supplant) the torah (his wisdom teachings will be taken up in another chapter). Like Zealots, Jesus and John found the temple situation to be intolerable and sought to change it, although not through violent revolution (violence too will be taken up later). And like the Essenes, Jesus and John sought to create an alternative system to the temple. That is what we will focus on now.

THE ESSENES AND PREFIGURATIVE POLITICS

Josephus describes the Essenes at great length in chapter 8, book 2 of *Jewish War*. Two other contemporary writers, the Hellenic-Jewish Philo of Alexandria and Roman philosopher Pliny the Elder, also mentioned them. We will take them in that order.

Josephus's accounts are extensive. While the Essenes are mentioned in *Antiquities*, *Jewish War* provides the bulk of Josephus's information about them so we'll stick with that. Below are the details most pertinent to our present inquiry.

Josephus writes that the Essenes are particularly disciplined "and seem to have a greater affection for one another than the other sects have." They propagate by recruiting new members and wed and procreate sparingly;

they seem to have been misogynistic, believing that women were inherently adulterous. They despised riches and lived communally: "It is a law among them, that those who come to them must let what they have be common to the whole order." They dressed in all white, which is a more important detail than it may appear (keep it in mind for a while). They regarded Moses most highly of all biblical figures aside from God himself. They purified themselves with water and ate together as a group. Josephus admired them for their piety, calling it "very extraordinary." He also reports that some of them attempted to divine the future by way of studying Scripture and purifying themselves (presumably through immersion) and "it is but seldom that they miss in their predictions." They believed strongly in fate and predestination, something that put them at odds with the Sadducees. Finally, there was "another order of Essenes," identical in every way except that they were more open to marriage, as long as there was a three-year engagement beforehand and its purpose was strictly procreation. This last bit is important because it illustrates the diversity inherent in not only the Essene community, but within any school of thought within Second Temple Judaism. None of them were a monolith.

Philo, an aristocratic Hellenic Jew born in 20 BCE, described the Essenes in his philosophical treatise *Every Good Man Is Free*. The only major point of disagreement between he and Josephus is that Philo says that the Essenes avoided cities and lived only in small village communities; Josephus says that they did live in cities. Whichever is right, Philo corroborates Josephus's picture of the Essenes as communalistic, sharing all wealth and doing nothing for personal gain. Philo also says that they were very pious and did not believe in slavery. Finally, he confirms twice that the Essenes took all meals together (recall, if you will, what we learned earlier about meal practice in regards to Jesus).

Pliny the Elder's account of the Essenes is the shortest, but perhaps the most interesting. He is the only Gentile whose writing on the Essenes has survived (another Gentile philosopher, Dio Chrysostom, also appears to have mentioned the Essenes but we only know this secondhand, from his biographer Synesius). I give Pliny's entire paragraph on the Essenes; the context is a description of Judea. It reads:

> *On the west side of the Dead Sea, but out of range of the noxious exhalations of the coast, is the solitary tribe of the Essenes, which is remarkable beyond all the other tribes in the whole world, as it has no women and has renounced all sexual desire, has no money,*

PRACTICE

and has only palm trees for company. [Day after day, however, their numbers are fully recruited by multitudes of strangers that resort to them, driven thither to adopt their usages by the tempests of fortune, and wearied with the miseries of life.][54] *Thus through thousands of ages (incredible to relate), a race in which no one is born lives on forever; so prolific for their advantage is other men's weariness of life! Lying below them was formerly the town of Engedi.*

Some textual issues with this. Pliny was a Gentile and seems not to have had much of an interest in Jewish sects besides the Essenes. They are the only ones he mentions. He appears to have visited them and been taken in by their piety and extraordinary way of living. He also refers to them as a "race" and says they have existed for "thousands of ages" when the reality was more likely a few centuries at most.

Be that as it may, he corroborates most of the information from Josephus and Philo. However, he adds that people were attracted to them because they offered an alternative to the miseries of ordinary life. Pliny wouldn't have written or understood this, but the political and material situation in Palestine certainly played a role in those miseries.

Pliny also fixes his Essenes in a single location, no doubt because these were the Essenes that he himself actually met or had been told about, on the west side of the Dead Sea, north of Ein Gedi (which is now a nature reserve).

This would be a relatively unremarkable tidbit (so some Essenes lived on the northwest side of the Dead Sea in an unimportant part of Judea—so what?) if not for a group of Bedouin shepherds who stumbled into a cave and discovered seven ancient scrolls inside jars near the Qumran archaeological site, on the northwest side of the Dead Sea. The story of the discovery, excavation, and eventual publication of the Dead Sea Scrolls is long and full of intrigue (not to mention decades of petty academic squabbling), but the scrolls themselves have provided a surfeit of information about Second Temple Judaism (the documents are all dated to the Second Temple period, including some from the first century CE), and, importantly for us, the Essenes.

The Scrolls certainly belonged to a community that lived at nearby Qumran. Many of the documents (there are at least fragments of over 800 individual documents) describe the ritual and practical practices of this

---

54. I have mostly used the translation by Harris Rackham for its simplicity; however, for the bracketed sentence I have used that by John Bostock. Bostock's translation better conveys the point I want to highlight about this section.

community. For decades after the initial discovery of the Scrolls, the scholarly consensus of their Essenic identity was so strong that it was practically taken for granted, to the point that "Essene" and "Qumran" could be used interchangeably. Recently this truism has been challenged[55] but scholarly consensus remains in favor of the "Essene hypothesis."

While I agree that it is never good to take these matters for granted, in my opinion the evidence is overwhelming that the Qumran community was comprised of Essenes or, minimally, an ideological offshoot of Essenes. I will briefly recount the main pieces of evidence that convinced me.

First is the corroboration with Pliny's account. This is most obvious and also the strongest. Pliny mentioned a community of Essenes living in this time and at this place. Frank Cross said in 1966 of this piece of evidence:

> *The scholar who would 'exercise caution' in identifying the sect of Qumran with the Essenes places himself in an astonishing position; he must suggest seriously that two major parties each formed communistic religious communities in the same district of the desert of the Dead Sea and lived together in effect for two centuries, holding similar bizarre views, performing similar or rather identical lustrations, ritual meals, and ceremonies. Further, the scholar must suppose that one community, carefully described by [Pliny the Elder], disappeared without leaving building remains or even potsherds behind; while the other community, systematically ignored by the classical sources, left extensive ruins and even a great library.*[56]

Next, the textual evidence itself. Many of the documents found in the caves near Qumran describe practices that are strikingly similar to what we know from our other sources about the Essenes. The Community Rule, one of the initial scrolls to be discovered, lays out many of the practices of the Qumran community.[57] Points of agreement between the contemporary accounts and the Community Rule include, with the corroborating author(s) in parenthesis:

---

55. See Boccaccini, *Beyond the Essene Hypothesis*, for an excellent discussion of the issues surrounding this. Boccaccini and those he cites as influences do not totally do away with the "Essene hypothesis"; rather their aim is to challenge some of its precepts in order to see the issue more holistically.

56. Cross, *Early History of the Qumran Community*, 77.

57. We can be relatively certain that the practices within correspond to the people living in the Qumran community because the archaeology corroborates it. For example, the Community Rule speaks of immersion in water as a purifying ritual; at Qumran have been found numerous ritual baths.

PRACTICE

- A high regard for Moses (Josephus)
- No private property (All)
- A belief in predestination (Josephus)
- All community members dined together (Philo and Josephus)
- Community members were ranked by experience (Philo and Josephus)
- They put a high value on knowledge and study (Philo and Josephus)
- Those wishing to join must go through a one-year trial period, followed by an even longer candidacy period (Josephus)
- They do not swear oaths (Philo and Josephus)

There are some minor discrepancies, but recall that Josephus even recognized multiple schools of thought within Essene Judaism. Other Dead Sea Scrolls provide further corroboration, but I don't want to belabor the point. I will just mention a final piece of evidence, which is archaeological.

Josephus mentioned that the Essenes dressed themselves in all white. It just so happens that every piece of textile found at Qumran happened to be white linen, which is highly unusual as most garments of this period were colorfully painted and wool, not linen, was the preferred textile in Judea.[58] Many of the Qumran linens had also been bleached white. Researchers concluded that the Qumran community "wished to differentiate themselves from the rest of the population also on the basis of their style of garments."[59]

I could go on. Study of the Dead Sea Scrolls and the Qumran community has become a discipline all to its own within the subject of Second Temple Judaism. That is not the point here, however; I have given as much information as I fear is necessary to justify my treating the Qumran community and their beliefs and practices as examples of Essenic Judaism or related to it.

Even if the Qumrans were not Essenes, or had split from the Essenes at some point over the course of their centuries-long history, they still provide corroborating evidence for a claim I want to make about the ministry of Jesus. This is necessary to counter the inevitable claim that I am being

---

58. Some wool textiles excavated from a nearby cave were later shown decisively *not* to be related to the Qumran settlement. See Sukenik and Shamir, "Qumran Textiles."

59. Sukenik and Shamir, "Qumran Textiles," 1.

anachronistic when I say that *Jesus's kingdom of God functioned as a prefigurative community.*

Prefigurative praxis (or politics) is the revolutionary act of creating the new type of world you envision within the existing world. The man who coined the term described it thusly: "By 'prefigurative,' I mean the embodiment, within the ongoing political practice of a movement, of those forms of social relations, decision-making, culture, and human experience that are the ultimate goal."[60] Or, as the Industrial Workers of the World puts it in their constitution: "forming the structure of the new society within the shell of the old."

The hyper-focus on the Essenic Qumran community is because I'm sure some fool will attack me for retrojecting a Marxist concept onto the Second Temple period. I reject this. Boggs and other modern communists may have given a name to this concept (Boggs even notes that it originated in nineteenth-century anarchist movements, not Marxist ones), but it has been a staple of millenarian and eschatological movements for millennia. It could be and was employed as a form of praxis by other devout Jews in the first century (the Qumrans and probably the Essenes as a whole), therefore it is at least a possibility that it was an element of Jesus's movement.

How else are we to understand the Community Rule's description of the Qumran community as "the ideal society of God"? They were clearly eschatological and apocalyptic; other scrolls such as the War Scroll describe a coming war between the "Sons of Light" and the "Sons of Darkness" after which God would have dominion over the earth (several elements of this are also found in the Community Rule, such as the Sons of Light and the rule of this world by Belial). Other, shorter texts, such as the New Jerusalem Scroll and the Book of Mysteries also allude to a unique eschatology. So they both expected a future ideal society of God, and saw their present community as that ideal society in embryo.

If the separation from larger Jewish communities, abstaining from sacrifice, and the performance of washing rituals for purity wasn't enough, textual evidence also makes it clear that the Qumran community, and probably the Essenes as a whole, had very negative views of the temple. Analysis led Ben Zion Wacholder to conclude that "authors of texts like the Heavenly Jerusalem, the Aramaic Testament of Levi, the book of Jubilees,

---

60. Boggs, *Marxism, Prefigurative Communism*, 2.

11QTorah, and [the Damascus Document] refused to recognize the legitimacy of the Second Temple."[61]

A key example that I stress comes from a fragmented letter found at Qumran, deemed 4QMMT. It is concerned with ritual practice and adherence to the Mosaic covenant, but it is hard to make specific judgments of what it originally said because it is so tattered. One of the more complete fragments we can piece together reads:

> *And also concerning the deaf who do not hear the law or the regulations concerning purity and do not hear the laws of Israel; for whoever neither sees nor hears, does not know how to behave; but these are approaching the purity of the temple.*[62]

First, this corroborates what I said earlier about "sinners" being those people systematically unable to access the temple's healing and purifying amenities, with a specific focus on blindness and deafness. The author(s) of 4QMMT are using them here not to make a point about sin or purity, but to mock the temple itself: the temple is only as pure as a blind or deaf man who does not know how to properly keep himself pure.

It can scarcely be more clear what was happening here. The Essenes believed the temple in Jerusalem to be corrupt (as many Jews did during the time of the Herodians and Rome). Their solution was to withdraw from the corrupt community and form the new eschatological community that they believed would supplant the present, corrupted world. They were apocalyptic as well as eschatological, believing that God would intervene with his heavenly hosts, kicking off a cosmic war in which the Sons of Darkness led by Belial (which means "wickedness" or "worthlessness" and was another name for Satan) would be defeated and the Messianic Age would begin. Whether they believed they were causing the divine intervention by instituting God's ideal kingdom, or merely preparing for its arrival, we cannot know with certainty, but there could have been differing views on it among different Essenes (which may help to explain why some eschewed marriage and others did not).

I stress: the Essenes/Qumrans did not *have* to prefiguratively create God's ideal society just because they viewed the temple as corrupt. There were a variety of responses to this contradiction. The fact that they did tells us with relative certainty, however, that it was an option.

---

61. Wacholder, "Ezekiel and Ezekielianism," 191.
62. 4QMMT lines 55, 56, 57.

I have already argued that Jesus was eschatological, but not apocalyptic. So despite many parallels between his thought and the Essenic teachings (which we will cover in the chapter on wisdom teachings), there were also some differences. I believe these differences can be elucidated by another concept from Marxist theory: dual power.

THE KINGDOM AS DUAL POWER

I argue that Jesus's ministry was prefigurative, like the Qumran community (and possibly the Essenes as a whole), of what he believed was God's ideal society. However, unlike the Qumran community, Jesus did not expect the kingdom to be brought about by divine intervention, but by human action. The Kingdom Movement was prefigurative, but it was also *revolutionary* in that it functioned as a form of dual power.

Vladimir Lenin first wrote of dual power in the wake of 1917's February Revolution, when the revolutionary coalition of Russia first ousted the Tsar.

> *The basic question of every revolution is that of state power. . . . The highly remarkable feature of our revolution is that it has brought about a dual power. . . . What is this dual power? Alongside the Provisional Government, the government of bourgeoisie, another government has arisen, so far weak and incipient, but undoubtedly a government that actually exists and is growing—the Soviets of Workers' and Soldiers' Deputies.*[63]

Lenin's dual power referred to a situation in which two separate state apparatuses functioned in competition with each other. One was the liberal government that seized power in February, the bourgeois government; and the other was the proletarian government-in-progress, typified by the soviets (worker's councils). Lenin theorized that under the proper leadership of the vanguard party (which he conceived of as his Bolshevik party), the worker's councils could emerge victorious and seize complete state power. He was proven right in October of that year when they did just that and the Soviet Union was born.

Since that time, "dual power" has evolved in meaning to refer to a conscious strategy of revolutionaries living under reactionary governments attempting to create a parallel state apparatus in order to win over

---

63. Lenin, *Dual Power*, 1.

PRACTICE

the masses to their cause by serving their interests where the bourgeois or reactionary state is failing. Chiapas, in Mexico, is a prime example; the Mexican government nominally holds power in the state, but the EZLN (Zapatista Army of National Liberation) has also set up institutions such as general and community assemblies, schools, hospitals, and worker cooperatives. They function separately from state-run or private institutions, and through them the Zapatistas have achieved massive popular support, especially among Chiapas's indigenous citizens.

And now we come back to John and his baptism for the forgiveness of sins on the Jordan River. We have seen that the nature of the temple created a class of permanently ritually impure people, people who simply could not keep to the Mosaic covenant regularly and so were looked down on by polite society as "sinners." John created not just a ritual, but an institution, especially for these people, subverting the temple authority in the same way that Zapatista schools subvert the Mexican government's authority.

But John's baptism didn't change anything about the temple on its own. If you recognized the temple as the only legitimate authority in the matter of forgiving sins, then it would not matter if a sinner had been baptized by John. Along with the new institution must come a prefigurative community willing to attach itself to that power. This, in my opinion, is where John failed and Jesus succeeded.

My argument is that the healing, forgiving, and eating aspects of Jesus's ministry focused as a form of prefigurative dual power in competition with and opposition to the second temple. We saw already that in its open commensality Jesus's movement embodied the radically egalitarian and communitarian social relations of the kingdom of God. The table is society in miniature, and the kingdom was a place where the table was seated with "the poor, the crippled, the blind, and the lame" (Luke 14:21b).

But Jesus went further. He combined this with the *dual power* aspect of John's movement, and by eschewing a fixed location in terms of a system of itinerant prophets, Jesus's new parallel institution of authority was able to cover more ground, reach more people, and form a real community that would outlast even himself.

The question now must arise: to what end? I have already laid out the reasons why I believe that Jesus, unlike John, did not base his movement around expectations of an imminent divine intervention. So then what did he believe would happen? What was the point of any of this?

Until now we have focused on Jesus's practice. To recap: Jesus's ministry, which we can call for convenience's sake the Kingdom Movement, was a system by which itinerant prophets, deputized by Jesus himself, would bring the good news to the poor and marginalized of Galilean society. They would heal the sick and declare their sins forgiven, and they had stunning success at treating the *illnesses* that were inherent to peasant life within Second Temple Judaism—ostracization, alienation, and general misery as a result of conditions beyond the peasant's control. They would come together with the people they ministered to in common meals, all members of this new Kingdom Movement sitting and eating together to model the new type of world Jesus wanted to create—a world of the sick, the poor, the disabled, the outcasts, all living and sharing together as equals.

This was the *practice* of the Kingdom Movement. In order to put it into context and understand it as *praxis*, we must now turn to the *theory* behind the Kingdom Movement. It is time at last to study Jesus's wisdom teachings.

Chapter 4

THEORY

If you want knowledge, you must take part in the practice of changing reality. If you want to know the taste of a pear, you must change the pear by eating it.... If you want to know the theory and methods of revolution, you must take part in revolution. All genuine knowledge originates in direct experience.

—Mao Tse-Tung

PRAXIS

The terms *theory* and *practice* form a dialectic that is resolved into *praxis*, which is simply the synthesis of theory and practice. When theory becomes practice, when practice refines theory, you have praxis.

We began with the practice of Jesus's ministry because, while it may seem counter-intuitive, practice actually precedes theory. Practice is the thesis, theory the antithesis, and praxis the synthesis. For example: Marxism is theory, but it was preceded by the practice of class struggle. Without millennia of class struggle, the theory of Marxism could never have been formulated. They were combined successfully into praxis for the first time in 1917 with the Bolshevik Revolution.

Jesus's practice did not exist apart from theory. Nor do I mean to suggest that he started doing it instinctively and only developed his theory later. His practice was living in Palestine in the first century, under the rule of imperialists and compradors. It was living as a Jew. It was living as a proletarian, a *tekton*. It was participating in John's ministry. Through all of this practice, Jesus developed his theory, which then manifested as the *praxis* of the Kingdom Movement.

I believe that it is actually necessary to begin with Jesus's practice before considering his teachings. As any Christian knows, almost any saying of Jesus's can be interpreted in various ways depending on your theological or political outlook. He did not write us a manifesto of his own words and thoughts; his words and teachings were collected later by different people, redacted, and come to us second-, third-, and even fourth-hand.

But by starting with practice, by examining what Jesus and his earliest followers actually did and what it would have meant to the people of his day, we are equipped to parse out the actual meaning behind his many ethical, spiritual, practical, and wisdom teachings. This is where many if not most historians of Jesus miss the mark: they fail see his teachings as informed dialectically by his practice. They assume that his teachings originated within his own mind, through studying the torah or meditating or listening to God or simply thinking hard about it, and then use the results of this exercise in futility to explain his practice, to wildly mixed results. This is idealism.

The materialist begins with practice, because practice is what deals with material reality. All of our inferences about Jesus thus far have been based around what he actually *did*, not what we think he believed based on something he might have said. With that framework, we can look at the words attributed to him in the gospels and better determine (a) if he actually said them; and (b) what they actually meant. While this still does not guarantee success, it is much harder for us now to read whatever we want to see into his teachings.

We will take his teachings by subject. Jesus taught in parables as well as direct commands, and he also interpreted and supplemented the torah just like the Pharisees did. All of his teachings must be understood within the context of the revolutionary community he was creating. Out of and through that deceptively complicated mission, he was able to give radical teachings about subjects as diverse as family, violence, wealth, God, rituals, hierarchy, ethics, leadership, and more. These are not universal precepts for living a good life, as so many Christians treat them today (if they even bother to consider Jesus's teachings at all). They are specific instructions and explanations relating to life within and without the kingdom of God, both in the present of Jesus's time and in the future when it was to overtake the wicked powers that be.

Lest you think again that I am simply taking terms like "praxis," "dialectical," and "theory" and retrojecting them onto Jesus because I want Jesus to have been a Marxist, we will begin with one of Jesus's most important teachings, a pair of sayings about knowledge itself that makes very clear how Jesus conceives of teaching and theory.

> *Beware of false prophets, who come to you in sheep's clothing but inwardly are ravenous wolves. You will know them by their fruits [καρπῶν]. Are grapes gathered from thorns, or figs from thistles? In the same way, every good tree bears good fruit, but the bad tree bears bad fruit. A good tree cannot bear bad fruit, nor can a bad tree bear good fruit. Every tree that does not bear good fruit is cut down and thrown into the fire.* (Matt 7:15–19)

This is a case where Matthew's redactions to this saying from Q (as well as *Thomas* 45) may actually help, rather than hinder, the meaning. Luke's and *Thomas's* versions lack the apocalyptic ending (which Matthew added).

> *No good tree bears bad fruit [καρπόν], nor again does a bad tree bear good fruit; for each tree is known by its own fruit. Figs are not gathered from thorns, nor are grapes picked from a bramble bush. The good person out of the good treasure of the heart produces good, and the evil person out of evil treasure produces evil; for it is out of the abundance of the heart that the mouth speaks.* (Luke 6:43–45)

The Luke/*Thomas* version is likely closer to what Jesus actually said (and Matthew adds the missing pieces from Luke's later, in ch. 12) but both mean the same thing. A teaching is only as good as the works that it produces, just as a tree is only as good as the fruit it produces. The "abundance of the heart" is a bad English translation; it's literal but not close to the intended meaning. A better one would be "it is out of the abundance of knowledge that the mouth speaks"; the heart was considered the source of knowledge in Aramaic-speaking culture, much like we might use the "brain" or "mind" today.[1] *Thomas's* version reflects this meaning.

---

1. Vermes, *Authentic Gospel of Jesus*, 102.

The bit about bearing good fruit has a parallel in the Parable of the Sower, which is attested in Mark (followed by Matthew and Luke) and *Thomas*. *Thomas*'s version is closest to the original:

> Now when the sower went out, took a handful [of seeds], and scattered them. Some fell on the road; the birds came and gathered them up. Others fell on the rock, did not take root in the soil, and did not produce ears. And others fell on thorns, they choked the seeds and worms ate them. And others fell on the good soil and it produced good fruit [καρπος]: it bore sixty per measure and a hundred and twenty per measure. (*Thomas* 9)

Now the *Gospel of Thomas* was originally written in Greek, however the only complete manuscript we have available is in Coptic, so the few Greek words (including "fruit" here) stand out. Again, the focus here is on the material produce, yet the key difference with the other parable is that there it is the *tree* which produces good or bad fruit, but here it is the *soil*, and only after being acted upon (spreading the seeds).

Mark adds a long-winded explanation of the Parable of the Sower immediately following its telling, which Matthew and Luke copy. Jesus takes his disciples aside, tells them that the purpose of teaching in parables is so that people may "look, but not perceive," and then spells out the meaning of every aspect of the parable for them. Matthew does this again for *The Planted Weeds*, which we have already discussed, and just as in that case with Matthew, Mark's explanation of the parable's meaning should be understood as his own interpretation of it, put onto the lips of Jesus.

This doesn't mean it's totally without merit. Mark includes again the genuine saying of Jesus about good fruit (which was a common aphorism Jesus employed, but did not invent). The seeds sown on good soil represent those who "hear the word and accept it and bear fruit" (Mark 4:20).

Mark's interpretation of the parable isn't terribly far off, but it does reflect the situation and needs of the early church, identifying the bad soils with flaky converts who abandon "the word" when facing persecution or hardship or else treat it as a fad, something to pass the time until they get distracted with "the cares of the world, and the desire for wealth, and the lures of other things" (Mark 4:18). In its original form the parable refers to the spreading of the gospel (the news that the kingdom of God was at hand), including the eating/exorcising mission we have already discussed. Jesus is teaching that this mission requires fertile ground to be successful, but that when it is successful it bears good fruits, manifests as action. Again we see the dialectic of practice and theory; each feeds the other.

Jesus's wisdom teachings, or his theory as I prefer to think of it, is no abstract exercise in interpreting Scripture. It is born of his and his comrades' experiences living as Jews under imperialism and class society. Never forget that faith without works is dead; not because works are required to justify faith, but because (for Paul as for James) there can be no true faith without works; works are the manifestation of faith just as praxis is the manifestation of theory.

THE KINGDOM

While we've already covered a lot of this ground in the section about apocalypticism, we will recap and expand here because this subject makes up an extensive portion of the corpus of Jesus's teachings, especially his parables. Additionally, even teachings not directly referencing the kingdom are still *about* some aspect of the kingdom, since the kingdom is the super-context of all Jesus said and did.

Many of Jesus's teachings about the kingdom take the form of simple simile-parables. *The kingdom is like X*, Jesus will say. Sometimes *X* is very concise, a short clause of only a few words. Other times it is a long and detailed metaphor with characters and narrative flow. Additionally, Jesus will sometimes speak directly about the kingdom, as is the case with the pericope about children (Mark 10:13–16, paralleled in Matthew 19, Luke 18, and *Thomas* 22). We'll start with the simpler parables attested in at least 2 sources. Here they all are, in their simplest formulations:

The Mustard Seed (Mark and Parallels; Thomas)

> *[The kingdom of God] is like a mustard seed, which, when sown upon the ground, is the smallest of all the seeds on earth; yet when it is sown it grows up and becomes the greatest of all shrubs, and puts forth large branches, so that the birds of the air can make nests in its shade. (Mark 4:30–32)*

The mustard seed was known in antiquity for being the tiniest of all seeds. The kingdom of God began as a tiny movement of Galilean peasants, but Jesus intended and expected it to grow until it overtook all of Judaism. This was an ideological apologetic against the charge that he and his small movement were nobody to challenge the authority of the temple and the ruling classes. Additionally, the kingdom is already present, tiny but steadily growing.

Seed and Sickle (Mark, Thomas)

> The kingdom of God is as if a man should scatter seed upon the ground, and should sleep and rise night and day, and the seed should sprout and grow, he knows not how. The earth produces of itself, first the blade, then the ear, then the full grain in the ear. But when the grain is ripe, at once he puts in the sickle, because the harvest has come. (Mark 4:26–29)

Matthew and Luke both leave this out, probably because they thought it was redundant with the longer Parable of the Sower, which Mark has right before this one. However, the final bit, about the sickle, appears independently (and in a totally different context) in saying 21 of *Thomas*, so it is likely that some of this does go back to the historical Jesus. As with the mustard seed, the kingdom is present and growing, even if those who "scattered the seeds" do not see it. The bit about the harvest sounds apocalyptic, although it could have originally referred to some second phase or culmination of the original Kingdom Movement that was never enacted before Jesus's death.

The Leaven (Q; Thomas)

> [The kingdom of God] is like yeast that a woman took and mixed in [literally: hid] with three measures of flour until all of it was leavened. (Luke 13:21 = Matt 13:33; Thomas 96)

The parable of the leaven continues the theme of the previous two; the kingdom is like yeast in bread, hidden but present and growing. One might ask: why so many parables with the same or similar themes? But that is precisely the great benefit of teaching in parables: their evocative and metaphorical language lends itself to multiple versions of the same teaching, helping listeners to draw comparisons and ponder on their own. They are an interactive form of teaching meant to evoke familiar situations; elucidate different aspects of the same thing; and invite interpretation.

The Pearl and The Treasure (Matthew, Thomas)

These are treated together because they are very similar and put in sequence by Matthew (Matt 13:44–46). The kingdom is like a fine pearl, or a treasure hidden in a field, and one should be prepared to give up all earthly possessions to purchase that pearl or that field. This need not be eschatological; the point isn't "the end is nigh, so sacrifice all your possessions," but rather: "the kingdom is worth all that you have." We must try to ask ourselves how Jesus's intended audience—poor Galilean peasants—would have listened to these parables. None of them would have had owned enough to sell for a precious pearl even if they did find one, and finding treasure buried in a field would be akin to winning the lottery today. Were Jesus's listeners imagining themselves selling their meager belongings to purchase a pearl? I think not. Fascinatingly, *Thomas*'s version of the Treasure ends with the lucky treasure-finder using his new riches to become a greedy money-lender, loaning out money "at interest to whomever he wished," a career forbidden by Mosaic law. Even if not the original version, *Thomas*'s version shows another way this parable could have been told or understood. We will come back to this proletarian reading of these parables when we cover Jesus's teachings on wealth.

Parable of the Rich Fool (Luke, Thomas)

> There was a rich person who had a great deal of money. He said, "I shall invest my money so that I may sow, reap, plant, and fill my storehouses with produce, that I may lack nothing." These were the very things he was thinking in his heart, but that very night he died. (*Thomas* 63; par. Luke 12:16–20)

Again *Thomas* preserves a simpler and likely more original version of a parable that Luke could not resist editorializing. There is no mention in either version of any kind of afterlife or apocalypse, so the original point of this parable is that riches and material wealth are not worth pursuing because life is finite.

The Weeds among the Wheat (Matthew, Thomas)

> The kingdom of the Father is like a man who had good seed. His enemy came by night and sowed weeds among the good seed. The

man did not allow them to pull up the weeds; he said to them, "I am afraid that you will go intending to pull up the weeds and pull up the wheat along with them." For on the day of the harvest the weeds will be plainly visible, and they will be pulled up and burned." (Thomas 57)

Matthew's version (13:24–30) is longer but narratively the same; he characteristically intensifies the apocalyptic elements. This is another one that Matthew interprets for us; his hyper-apocalyptic interpretation reflects his own (and his community's) perspective. The original core of this parable, if it goes back to Jesus (I am unsure), likely emphasized the good produce growing among the weeds more than the harvest itself; essentially it is a call to leave judgment to God. (There is another possible interpretation that we will save for later.)

The Great Banquet (Q, Thomas)

We are beginning to get into more complicated territory. The parable of the Great Banquet, as mentioned above in the section on *The Mission*, has been heavily redacted in different ways by both Matthew and Luke (from its original in Q). *Thomas*'s version is given here, because it is the simplest and likely closest to the original:

> *A man had received visitors. And when he had prepared the dinner, he sent his servant to invite the guests.*
>
> *He went to the first one and said to him, "My master invites you." He said, "I have claims against some merchants. They are coming to me this evening. I must go and give them my orders. I ask to be excused from the dinner."*
>
> *He went to another and said to him, "My master has invited you." He said to him, "I have just bought a house and am required for the day. I shall not have any spare time."*
>
> *He went to another and said to him, "My master invites you." He said to him, "My friend is going to get married, and I am to prepare the banquet. I shall not be able to come. I ask to be excused from the dinner."*
>
> *He went to another and said to him, "My master invites you." He said to him, "I have just bought a farm, and I am on my way to collect the rent. I shall not be able to come. I ask to be excused."*
>
> *The servant returned and said to his master, "Those whom you invited to the dinner have asked to be excused." The master said to his servant, "Go outside to the streets and bring back those whom*

> *you happen to meet, so that they may dine." Businessmen and merchants will not enter the places of my father.* (*Thomas* 64; synoptic versions in Matt 22:2–14; Luke 14:16–24)

Matthew's version of this parable is the only one to specify that the feast is for the wedding of a king's son; he interjects several bizarre and ill-fitting elements to the story including the murder of the king's servants by the invitees as well as a separate, independent saying about a wedding garment (probably not going back to the historical Jesus). None of this is original to the parable and clearly reflects the situation after the destruction of the temple in the year 70; Matthew's community believed that the second coming of Christ was very near.

Luke preserves most of the original narrative, but adds a second wave of invitees after the first is not enough. First it is "the poor and maimed and blind and lame," and when even this proves to not be enough the master commands his servants to "compel people to come in, that my house may be filled." Luke, who may have been a Gentile himself, clearly has the new Gentile church that was beginning to supplant the original Jewish membership of the early Christian community, in mind with this second batch of guests.

Behind these layers of redaction lies one of the most descriptive parables of the kingdom we have. *Thomas*'s appendix about "businessmen and merchants" coupled with Luke's identification of the original guests as the "poor and maimed and blind and lame" reflect the original meaning of the parable even if not the exact wording Jesus used (and he probably experimented with different ways of telling his parables). The kingdom was a great feast, a celebration, but it was not filled with the wealthy elites or high priests; the ruling classes had their chance to participate in the kingdom and spurned it. Now the kingdom was a place of the poor, the disabled, and the outcast. The servant or servants are Jesus and his followers, tasked with bringing these people into the kingdom through the *Mission*.

We will move away from parables for a moment to a few other sayings about the kingdom that do not fit the parable format. Other books on the historical Jesus usually group parables separately from so-called "wisdom sayings." I have chosen instead to treat Jesus's teachings by subject to allow these different forms of teaching to complement one another.

The Beatitudes (Q, Thomas [Partial])

The famous Beatitudes come to us in differently redacted versions in Matthew and Luke, with a few parallels spread out throughout *Thomas*. Matthew gives us several Beatitudes not found in Luke, while Luke adds three corresponding "woes" or curses after his three. We will start first with those attested by Matthew, Luke, and *Thomas*.

> *Blessed are the poor, for theirs is the kingdom.* (Thomas 54; Matt 5:3; Luke 6:20)
>
> *Blessed are you who are hungry now, for you will be filled.* (Luke 6:21; Matt 5:6; Thomas 69b)
>
> *Blessed are you when people revile you and persecute you and utter all kinds of evil against you on my account. Rejoice and be glad, for your reward is great in heaven.* (Matt 5:11–12; Luke 6:22–23; Thomas 68–69a)

I do not share the view of some New Testament scholars that these are the *only* Beatitudes that go back to the historical Jesus; however we will treat them here for the sake of methodology, recognizing that the Beatitudes have been heavily redacted by each author who transmits them and a perfect reconstruction is probably impossible to make.

The first to note is that Luke and *Thomas* agree against Matthew on the material nature of the "poor" and "hungry." Matthew has qualified these people as the "poor in spirit" and "those who hunger and thirst for righteousness." Matthew's aims were probably not nefarious, but his redactions are clearly later.

Next, the word "blessed" must be carefully understood. The Scholars' Translation of the Bible created by the Fellows of the Jesus Seminar changes it to "congratulations" and Burton Mack renders it as "how fortunate."[2] Both are dynamic equivalencies, expressing the idea behind the statement rather than the literal meaning. "Blessed" is often understood passively, as a state of being or as something that has already happened. To say that the poor, hungry, and persecuted are blessed should be understood more as a proclamation, much like proclaiming that somebody's sins have been forgiven. It is, in effect, the "good news" that Jesus speaks so often of.

The woes and curses make explicit what is implied anyway by the positive blessings.

---

2. Mack, *Lost Gospel*.

> *But woe to you who are rich, for you have received your consolation. Woe to you who are full now, for you will be hungry. Woe to you who are laughing now, for you will mourn and weep.* (Luke 6:24–25)

The theme here is one of reversal: the poor are blessed while the rich are cursed. Or, the poor have good news brought to them (Matt 11:4 = Luke 7:22) and the rich have bad news brought to them.

This is crucial because modern Christianity has made the message of Jesus into a universal proclamation. Jesus came to preach good news to the poor and hungry, but also to *condemn* the rich and well fed. This recalls a phrase which appears many times in slight alterations in Mark, Q, and *Thomas*: "The last will be first, and the first will be last."

To restate: The Beatitudes in their original form served as an encapsulation of what is meant by the word "gospel"—the good news. They were, in effect, the manifesto of the Kingdom Movement, signaling the dramatic reversal of fortunes that the kingdom would bring. The poor would be first while the rich would be brought low; the hungry would be fed and the well-fed would be left hungry; and those who were persecuted would find justice. Never forget that in any class society wealth cannot exist without exploitation, and good news to one class is necessarily bad news to another class.

The Kingdom and Wealth

Here again we see the exclusivity of the kingdom put in specific terms. A rich young man asks Jesus what he must do to "inherit eternal life" (synonymous with joining the kingdom). Jesus tells him to follow the torah, to which the rich man replies that he always has. Jesus's reply is one of his most stunning and radical sayings:

> *Jesus, looking at him, loved him and said, "You lack one thing; go, sell what you own, and give the money to the poor, and you will have treasure in heaven; then come, follow me." When he heard this, he was shocked and went away grieving, for he had many possessions.*
>
> *Then Jesus looked around and said to his disciples, "How hard it will be for those who have wealth to enter the kingdom of God!" And the disciples were perplexed at these words. But Jesus said to them again, "Children, how hard it is to enter the kingdom of God! It is easier for a camel to go through the eye of a needle than for someone*

who is rich to enter the kingdom of God." (Mark 10:21–25; par. Matt 19; Luke 18)

This saying is straightforward, despite the attempts of rich Christians to twist it so that rich people don't feel unwelcome in church. Wealth is simply incompatible with the kingdom of God, and those of great wealth must renounce it if they wish to enter the Kingdom Movement. This is echoed elsewhere, such as in *Thomas* 110. Again we have clear evidence that the kingdom was a movement of the poor and propertyless, *against* the wealthy.

One might ask whether this command is something that was actually practiced or expected to be practiced, or some sort of metaphorical flourish or pious thought. Jesus probably did not say this statement in response to a specific young wealthy man, but as an instruction to wealthy would-be disciples. So the question is, how serious was it?

Two pieces of evidence lead me to conclude that this command was taken very seriously and very literally.

First, it is followed by a brief dialogue where the disciples remark that it seems impossible for anyone to enter the kingdom; Jesus replies that all things are possible with God. This is obviously a later creation and doesn't even make sense if you give it any thought. Jesus's original statement doesn't imply that it would be difficult for anybody to enter the kingdom except rich people. Mark is editorializing, and this makes the best sense in the context of Christianity attracting middle- and upper-class converts, and nobody wanting to upset them. This presupposes that the original command was taken seriously at some point.

Another piece of evidence is in Acts (and so a separate source). After the death of Jesus, Luke reports that his disciples went to Jerusalem and formed a commune.

> *Now the whole group of those who believed were of one heart and soul, and no one claimed private ownership of any possessions, but everything they owned was held in common. . . . There was not a needy person among them, for as many as owned lands or houses sold them and brought the proceeds of what was sold. They laid it at the apostles' feet, and it was distributed to each as any had need.* (Acts 4:32–35)

This differs from Jesus's command in one important way. In Acts, new believers donate all of their possessions to a common treasury. Jesus, on the other hand, did *not* tell the rich man to distribute his wealth among everyone in the Kingdom Movement. The command is specifically to give all of his wealth away to "the poor," and *then* enter the kingdom. The kingdom has no need for a treasury, for it is meant to be reliant on the masses. It is a movement of the poor, by the poor. This clear development points to the originality of Jesus's command.

Based on this, I conclude that disposal of all private property was an absolute requirement *before* one could join the Kingdom Movement. Building on this, we can surmise the class composition of the movement itself.

Peasants are obvious—they made up the vast majority of free people in the time of Jesus. The classical world was overwhelmingly an agrarian world, with agricultural production making up the majority of production. Galilee was largely a rural region, and the pastoral and agricultural setting of most of Jesus's parables reflects this. However, during Jesus's life Galilee was urbanizing as Antipas rebuilt Sepphoris and built the great new city of Tiberias to impress the emperor of the same name. This necessitated a large urban workforce, a mix of slaves and free laborers such as *tektons*—builders—which the gospels tell us Jesus was:

> *Is not this the carpenter* [τέκτων], *the son of Mary and brother of James and Joses and Judas and Simon, and are not his sisters here with us?"* (Mark 6:3; par. Matt 13:55)

That Greek word—*tekton*—is usually translated as "carpenter" which in popular usage implies artisanal craftsmanship. We like to imagine Jesus as painstakingly crafting fine furniture or even art, like a middle-class American artisan. However, carpenter should be understood much more broadly, as indeed it is professionally in modern times. Carpenters are workers who build buildings: walls, flooring, windows, doors, roofing, etc. (our word archi*tect* comes from it). And *tekton* does not even necessarily imply woodworking—it could also mean stonemasonry, and indeed archaeological excavations of Nazareth have shown that it supported a sizeable stonecutting industry for such a small town.[3] The criterion of embarrassment makes this a reliable bit of data—Matthew is clearly embarrassed by Jesus's status as a *tekton*, and so here Jesus is merely "the carpenter's son"—presumably Joseph is the carpenter here. Yet in a world where sons usually followed in their fathers' footsteps, even this would not do for Luke, who ignores this fact about Jesus.

---

3. Bockmuehl, *Cambridge Companion to Jesus*, 14.

So Jesus was likely a builder, a manual laborer. In a world where much or even most manual labor was done by slaves, free laborers were rarely guaranteed steady work every day (see Jesus's parable of the workers in the vineyard as an example). They were *below* peasants in the class hierarchy, as even peasants could rely on the land they either owned or rented (and land ownership was a part of Yahweh's original covenant with the Israelites—each family was allotted their own land). Jesus's lower-class status was embarrassing to the early Christians, who successively downplayed it in the gospel tradition, as they did with numerous other unseemly bits of information about their savior.

So it is natural that these working-class people—the peasants and the proletariat, were among those who Jesus brought his message to. To them he added a special concern for those whom today we would call the lumpenproletariat—these are the "sinners" we have already spoken of, people excluded from the regular economy and polite society, the "shady" people, the people that upstanding citizens did not associate with.

This was the class composition of the Kingdom Movement. It is no surprise that anyone wealthy was required to dispose of all of their wealth first. You cannot have a community of equals where some are rich and others are destitute.

The Kingdom and Children (Mark, Thomas)

> *Truly I tell you, whoever does not receive the kingdom of God as a little child will never enter it. (Mark 10:15)*
>
> *These nursing babies are like those who enter the kingdom. (Thomas 22a)*

Saying 22 of *Thomas* then has the disciples essentially repeat Jesus's statement about babies back to him as a question, which leads into a rather abstract speech about contradictions. Personally I believe some of this does go back to the historical Jesus because he did think in contradiction and paradox, and one piece of it has a parallel in Galatians, but in any case this is a tenuous suggestion and it has nothing to do with the original saying about children.

There are two themes at play here. One is humility, which will be touched on soon. The other is trust and dependence. Children depend on their parents just as members of the kingdom are supposed to depend on and trust each other as well as God, their Father (see Matt 23:9).

More on family and fatherhood will be said later. For now, the point is that those wishing to join the Kingdom Movement must be innocent, trusting, and hopeful, like children. These qualities would be necessary in a movement as radical and ambitious as the Kingdom Movement was.

Light, Secrecy, Generosity (Mark and Parallels; Thomas [Partial])

Is a lamp brought in to be put under the bushel basket, or under the bed, and not on the lampstand? For there is nothing hidden, except to be disclosed; nor is anything secret, except to come to light. . . . Pay attention to what you hear; the measure you give will be the measure you get, and still more will be given to you. For those who have, more will be given; and from those who have nothing, even what they have will be taken away. (Mark 4:21–25)

This block of material is actually a grouping of four separate sayings that Mark put together, probably because they are thematically similar. Matthew and Luke rearrange the units, and *Thomas* contains three of them (lacking only the bit about "the measure you give").

The beginning, about light, may as well be included in his teachings about teaching; the good news of the kingdom is like a light that is meant to be displayed. Within the kingdom all secrets are to be made manifest; this directly contradicts Mark's assertion that the purpose of teaching in parables was to conceal the truth. That is redaction; this is reality. Parables are meant to inspire questioning and invite interpretation, but not to deceive or conceal. Jesus clearly believed that what he was teaching was important and meant to be understood.

The latter sayings also allude to Jesus's idiosyncratic notions of fairness within the kingdom. "The measure you give" pericope probably also appeared in Q, for both Matthew and Luke have it following the maxim "Do not judge, lest you be judged" (Matt 7:1; Luke 6:37. Luke splits it from the line "Pay attention to what you hear," which he leaves where it is in Mark). Teachings on behavior will be taken up later, but this continues to the astonishing claim that "whoever has something in his hand will receive more, and whoever has nothing will be deprived of even the little he has" (*Thomas* 41).

Taken at face value, this seems to fly in the face of everything we think we know about the kingdom. Does the kingdom not constitute a reversal of fortunes? But this seems to suggest an intensification of the existing situation. The answer lies in the language itself. It is a peculiar example of antithetical parallelism; the contrast between two opposite things, one positive and one negative, with intent to focus on the positive aspect. It is a common feature in the Hebrew Bible:

> *Words spoken by the wise bring them favor, but the lips of fools consume them.* (Eccl 10:12)

The technique is often used for poetic effect, especially in the Psalms:

> *The righteous shall be kept safe forever, but the children of the wicked shall be cut off.* (Ps 37:28)

Jesus was using a modified version of antithetical parallelism as a rhetorical flourish to illustrate the abundance within the kingdom. There are other examples of him doing this:

> *Is it lawful to do good or to do harm on the sabbath, to save life or to kill?* (Mark 3:1–2)

This saying obviously has its own context within the complex of sayings about healing as well as adherence to Mosaic law, but for now doesn't it strike you as odd that Jesus asks if it is lawful to kill on the Sabbath? Something that is never lawful? It is obviously a rhetorical question meant to draw attention to the true issue about whether it is lawful to save life.

Another example: in the Sermon on the Mount, Matthew has Jesus say: "You have heard that it was said, 'You shall love your neighbor and hate your enemy'" (Matt 5:43). The former clause—*you shall love your neighbor*—is a reference to Leviticus 19:18. But Matthew adds the opposite, *you shall hate your enemy*, even though this is not actually a commandment anywhere in the Hebrew Bible. Matthew was Jewish and obviously knew that; this addition is a rhetorical flourish not meant to be taken literally.

So it is with this troublesome parable about he who has nothing somehow losing more than what he has. It is characteristic of Jesus's creative and dialectical mind, and again we ask ourselves how his poor listeners would have heard it. The teaching emphasizes the abundance of the kingdom, but does so through an absurdity—and Jesus's listeners definitely would have understood the absurdity. This was a part of the radicality of the kingdom. Bear it in mind as we move back to parables.

THEORY

The Workers of the Vineyard (Matthew 20:1–6)

This parable is long, so I will recap rather than reproduce it. A householder goes out early in the morning to hire day laborers to work his vineyard. He offers to pay them a denarius for a full day's work, the standard wage. He goes back out a few hours later and hires more workers, and then several more times throughout the day, all the way until "the eleventh hour" when the workday is nearly over. At the end he pays all of the workers the exact same wage, whether they worked the entire twelve hours or just a single hour at the end. When the workers who had been there the longest complain, he tells them that he is paying them what they agreed upon and that it is fair regardless of what he chooses to pay the others.

This parable is only in Matthew, but it is characteristic of Jesus's way of thought. It is a parable that I personally struggled with when trying to understand Jesus's ministry as revolutionary praxis; shouldn't all be compensated according to their contribution? That is certainly the orthodox Marxist view (while allowing for "from each according to their ability," of course). But Jesus's vision is even *more* radical; wealth is to be shared absolutely equally. The kingdom is a state of abundance, but also of complete equality. Perhaps not *fairness* the way we traditionally understand it—but equality.

Like any good parable, the Workers of the Vineyard is not limited to this surface-level reading. It is not just that the kingdom is a place of total equality—the message is also that the purpose of joining the kingdom is not for personal gain. Joining now won't net you any more reward than joining later—because nobody should be coming into the kingdom for the rewards. Not for money, status, popularity, or any other form of capital. This points to another theme of Jesus's movement that we have seen in practice, and will consider soon as theory: the emphasis on *serving*, on members of the kingdom as *servants*.

The Lost Sheep (Q, Thomas)

> *The kingdom is like a shepherd who had a hundred sheep. One of them, the largest, went astray. He left the ninety-nine and looked for the one until he found it. After he had toiled, he said to the sheep, "I love you more than the ninety-nine." (Thomas 107)*

> *What do you think? If a shepherd has a hundred sheep, and one of them has gone astray, does he not leave the ninety-nine on the mountains and go in search of the one that went astray? And if he finds it, truly I tell you, he rejoices over it more than over the ninety-nine that never went astray. So it is not the will of your Father in heaven that one of these little ones should be lost.* (Matt 18:12–14)

Luke's version is typically verbose, but substantively the same. *Thomas* adds the unnecessary detail that it was the "largest" sheep that left, but this simple parable is likely one that Jesus employed often. The kingdom is a place where redemption is possible. It is the duty of the shepherds of the kingdom (Jesus and his followers) to find those who have strayed away from God's radical community and bring them into the movement. It is reminiscent of another saying, originally from Mark:

> *Those who are well have no need of a physician, but those who are sick; I have come to call not the righteous but sinners.* (Mark 2:17)

Here again is the connection between sin and sickness, as well as the proclamation that it is the unhealthy and the unclean—the "lost sheep"—that are the focus of Jesus's ministry.

There are a few things I take away from all of the above sayings about the nature of the kingdom and Jesus's teachings. The first is that his parables generally utilize the imagery and motifs of the countryside—vineyards, agriculture, animal husbandry, etc. This makes sense as his target audience was rural people, but it also gives us another criterion with which to judge other sayings, and especially parables. Are they pastoral, agricultural? Or cosmopolitan, urban? The former are more likely (although not always) to go back to Jesus, while the latter are more likely (but still not always!) to be the creation of later thinkers.

More importantly, if Jesus has done his job correctly, we are beginning to think about the kingdom in multiple different ways. We understand who it is there for—not only the outcasts, but especially those who have gone astray. It is a place of forgiveness and redemption, but also of total equality. It challenges our notions of fairness, and asks that we let go of our attachments to material wealth. Bear all of this in mind as we move from general to specific and consider sayings that hone in on certain aspects of the kingdom, such as servitude.

THEORY
A KINGDOM OF SERVANTS

A theme that appears often in the teachings of Jesus is servitude. Jesus both declares that his role is as a servant and instructs his followers, those entering into the Kingdom Movement, that they should become servants. We have already seen this in places such as the parable of the Great Banquet; it is the servants tasked with bringing the dregs of society into the great feast that is the kingdom. Jesus alludes to it in numerous "wisdom sayings" such as Mark 9:35 (paralleled in a different context in Matt 23:11). In Mark's version, Jesus is responding to an argument the Twelve were having about which was the greatest among them. "Whoever wants to be first must be last of all and servant of all," Jesus tells them. Matthew puts his modified version of the saying within a complex of sayings from Mark and Q that in its final form amounts to an unhinged rant against "scribes and Pharisees" that certainly does not go back to the historical Jesus in this form.

Another related saying comes from Mark and is copied by Matthew and Luke.

> *You know that among the Gentiles those whom they recognize as their rulers lord it over them, and their great ones are tyrants over them. But it is not so among you: whoever wishes to become great among you must be your servant, and whoever wishes to be first among you must be servant of all. [For who is greater, the one who is at the table or the one who serves? Is it not the one at the table? But I am among you as one who serves.]* (Mark 10:42–44 [Luke 22:27]; par. Matt 20)

Mark adds after this an ill-fitting line about the Son of Man giving his life "as ransom for many," which is the creation of the post-Easter church. The context here again is a dispute among The Twelve, this time about which will get to sit beside Jesus after the second coming. This is a common theme when dealing with The Twelve; Jesus is often portrayed as giving instructions specifically to them. This is unlikely to have actually been the case. When the gospels as we have them today were being composed and collected after what is rightly called the Apostolic Age (from the death of Jesus to the death of the last of the Twelve), The Twelve were seen as important authority figures. This importance and authority was retrojected by the gospel authors onto the life of the historical Jesus, but the differing accounts of who they were and what their names are, along with the fact that as we have already seen the Kingdom Movement was built on a system of itinerant prophets that could not have been limited to only twelve (or even seventy in Luke) people tells us that the Twelve was likely a fluid group whose membership changed during the course of Jesus's life. He probably did select twelve apostles to hold a somewhat special place in his movement, and the number—twelve—symbolizes the Twelve Tribes of Israel. But it is unlikely that most of his teachings directed at the Twelve specifically were originally meant only for them. Were this the case, it is unlikely many of them would have survived. Most likely their selection was a prophetic and symbolic action meant to recall the Twelve Tribes and their function was to act as leadership when Jesus was not around as well as learn and repeat his teachings to others.

So we should understand these and other commands as relating to all members of the Kingdom Movement, not just the Twelve. They were in a position of leadership, but they were also servants, like Jesus himself. Again we see the fondness of contradiction characteristic of Jesus's thought.

All of this helps to contextualize another, similar yet distinct teaching—humility. *"Whoever exalts himself will be humbled, and whoever humbles himself will be exalted,"* Jesus says in Q (Matt 23:12; Luke 14:11; 18:14).

Why the emphasis on servitude? Apart from any concrete practice, it might seem as though Jesus is preaching a banal humility, or an ethical instruction to be kind and help others for the sake of doing so. Since we started with practice, however, we know better.

In the context of the mission to the poor and outcast of rural Galilee, the purpose of which was the creation of a new dual power institution of healing that was prefigurative of the coming kingdom of God, the emphasis on serving can be understood in revolutionary terms. In fact, it is Jesus's version of another concept found often in modern radical movements. Serving within the kingdom of God amounted to what we today would call mass work.

"Serving the people" was one of the primary methods by which the Communist Party of China achieved mass support and eventual victory during the Chinese Civil War of the 1940s. It was a hallmark of the political theory of Mao Zedong, and that legacy is carried on today in Maoist formations across the world.

Mao thought that revolutionaries should distinguish themselves from other political entities by their unceasing servitude to the people's interests. Mao explained it best in a 1934 speech at the Second National Congress of Workers' and Peasants' Representatives:

THEORY

> *We must . . . solve the problems facing the masses—food, shelter and clothing, fuel, rice, cooking oil and salt, sickness and hygiene, and marriage. In short, all the practical problems in the masses' everyday life should claim our attention. If we attend to these problems, solve them and satisfy the needs of the masses, we shall really become organizers of the well-being of the masses, and they will truly rally round us and give us their warm support.*[4]

Now obviously I am not trying to claim that Jesus intended the Kingdom Movement to culminate in a mass uprising or violent revolution—there simply isn't enough positive data to make that argument. I am saying, however, that Jesus wanted to bring in as many of "the lost sheep of the House of Israel" into his movement as he could, and recognized that the best way to do that was to attend to the peoples' material and spiritual needs (hence the eating and healing). To clarify: Jesus did *not* want his movement to be as big as possible; it was exclusive to the types of people Mao would call "the masses"—peasants and workers, as well as those left out of the regular economy that we would today call the lumpenproletariat (the prostitutes, lepers, "sinners," etc.). We will say more about this later.

For an example a bit closer to home for Western readers, think of the Black Panther Party's (who were inspired by Mao) Free Breakfast for Children program. Recognizing the government's inability and unwillingness to make breakfast available to students in inner-city schools, the Panthers instituted their own breakfast programs in cities across America, serving free food to thousands of schoolchildren every morning. This act of service eventually shamed the federal government into instituting its own breakfast programs, as well as helped the Panthers to gain mass support in poor black communities.

I emphasize—this was *not* charity. They did not do it simply because it was the "right thing to do." Elaine Brown explains the reasoning behind the free breakfast program in her autobiography, *A Taste of Power*:

> *The potency of the Panther "Comm-uh-nis" threat lay not so much in the puny Panther guns, [J. Edgar] Hoover had warned America, as in the "butter" the Panthers were spreading over the minds of the ignorant black masses, Panther propaganda promoted as social programs for the poor.*
>
> *Hoover had, in a manner of speaking, hit the nail on the head. The more the party sharpened the contradictions between haves and the have-nots, between the powerful and the powerless, the oppressor*

---

4. Mao, *Selected Works*, vol. 1.

and the oppressed, the more the people would seek to resolve them. That . . . was precisely the purpose of the party's Free Breakfast for Children program.[5]

Service to the people was a revolutionary strategy to bring class consciousness to the masses. It was a part of their long-term revolutionary goal of overthrowing the United States, defeating the capitalist economic system, and liberating black people from the yoke of white supremacy.

The Kingdom Movement had similar aims—the removal of the unjust powers of Rome and its collaborators, and the institution of a new order called the kingdom of God. I have already argued that a divine, cataclysmic culmination where God would dramatically sweep away those evil powers and replace them with new ones was *not* what the Kingdom Movement expected. So then what did they expect? Was it to be violent, or nonviolent? That is our next, difficult topic.

NOT PEACE, BUT A SWORD?

The question of Jesus's views on violence is dangerous territory on which to tread, for the popular view of Jesus as a total pacifist is so widely accepted and taken for granted that daring to question it, even mildly, invites criticism that one is engaging in historical revisionism of the worst kind, or simply trying to get attention by making an outrageous claim.

I am doing neither here. Because this is such a controversial subject, I will be as clear as I can from the very beginning: I reject the so-called "Zealot hypothesis," that theory that aligns Jesus primarily with the Zealots who rose up in arms against the Romans in the year 66. I have already stated that Jesus did have some similarities with the Zealots—namely the desire to see the political and religious authorities removed and replaced with something different—but the Kingdom Movement differed from Zealotry in its tactics as well as what it believed would be replacing the current, unjust powers.

With that said, I *also* reject the simplistic and reductive view of Jesus as a peacenik, a staunch pacifist à la Gandhi. Jesus's views of violence and its place in the Kingdom Movement are more complicated than most people want to think about, as shown by a careful analysis of the relevant data.

---

5. Brown, *Taste of Power*, 156.

On the one hand, Jesus does seem to excoriate violence in many sayings. He orders a disciple (Peter in John, but unnamed in Matthew) to "put your sword back into its place; for all who take the sword will perish by the sword" (Matt 26:52; John's version lacks the instruction that all who take by the sword will perish by it). In the gospel context, Jesus is ordering his followers not to defend him from arrest because he must be arrested and executed "so that the scriptures of the prophets may be fulfilled" (Matt 26:56). Because this context is clearly the creation of the later church, and the fact that "all who take the sword will perish by the sword" has no parallels, I do not think it goes back to the historical Jesus. However, there are other sayings ("turn the other cheek," "do not resist evil," etc.) that are harder to dispose of, so a nonviolent attitude is certainly in the cards.

Those aforementioned sayings as well as other relevant pericopes are found within the so-called "Sermon on the Mount" in Matthew chapters 5 through 7 (and their Lukan parallels, making them from Q), and fall under the category of "rules of behavior," a sort of manual of discipline for members of the Kingdom Movement. This will be our next subject. For now, it will be instructive to consider the larger context in which the gospels were written.

To recap: the earliest gospel, Mark, was written in the wake of the destruction of Jerusalem and the end of the first Romano-Jewish war in the year 70 CE. The Christian Jews, by and large, did not take part in this war, which was led by the Zealot faction. We can see this in the story of Barabbas, during Jesus's execution.

In his Passion Narrative (from which Luke and Matthew get theirs), Mark says: "At the festival [Pilate] used to release a prisoner for them, anyone for whom they asked" (15:6). This detail leads into the story of the crowd of Jews, spurred on by the high priests, selecting a rebel named Barabbas to be pardoned instead of Jesus. Barabbas is specifically "in prison with the rebels who had committed murder during the insurrection" (15:7).

This story is entirely Mark's creation (or the creation of whoever wrote the Passion Narrative that Mark used). We will discuss the Passion Narrative in its entirety shortly, but this small unit on its own does not pass even a cursory historical analysis. There is no evidence whatsoever of a tradition of pardoning a prisoner during Passover or any festival, and the idea that Pilate, a man so brutal and chauvinistic against the Jews that he was recalled from his post for his cruelty, respecting their festivals and pardoning murderers for them is quite frankly absurd. The story is allegorical and reflects a Christian polemic against non-Christian Jews in the wake of the destruction of Jerusalem: they chose the rebel Barabbas over the Messiah Jesus, and see how that worked out for them?

This was the dominant attitude of the Jewish Christian community at the end of the first century CE—that violent revolt had led to the destruction of Jerusalem and this was a result of the failure of most Jews to accept the messiahship of Jesus. In the wake of this failure, it was natural for them to want to distance themselves and the founder of their movement from the Zealot attitude toward violence by any means necessary, including by inventing or twisting Jesus's teachings to seem more pacifistic than they may have been.

It is against this backdrop that "those who take by the sword will perish by the sword" must be seen. The Jews had taken by the sword and many of them had perished by it. The Jewish Christians who wrote and transmitted the gospels were eager to differentiate themselves to a battered and confused populace in search of an answer to why God had not made them victorious against the Romans.

This does not mean, however, that Jesus preached violent revolution. One saying certainly seems to point in that direction, found in Q and *Thomas*.

> *Do not think that I have come to bring peace to the earth; I have not come to bring peace, but a sword.* (Matt 10:34)

Luke's version of this saying (12:51) confirms my earlier point, about the early Christians distancing Jesus from violence as time goes on; he removes the reference to a sword and replaces it with "division." *Thomas's* version, however, includes the sword *as well as* division.

> *Men think, perhaps, that it is peace which I have come to cast upon the world. They do not know that it is dissension which I have come to cast upon the earth: fire, sword, and war. For there will be five in a house: three will be against two, and two against three, the father against the son, and the son against the father. And they will stand solitary.* (*Thomas* 16)

The succeeding context, however, makes it clear that Jesus is referring to division within the family. Family is such an important subject of Jesus's teaching that it deserves its own section. For now we see only that Jesus thought that the divisiveness of his teachings would perhaps manifest as violence.

THEORY

Another saying from Q is perhaps illustrative. "From the days of John the Baptist until now the kingdom of heaven has suffered violence, and the violent take it by force," says Jesus in Matthew 11:12. Luke 16:16 has a slightly different version; here it reads, "The law and the prophets were in effect until John came; since then the good news of the kingdom of God is proclaimed, and everyone tries to enter it by force."

The same Greek word, βιάζεται (*biazetai*), is translated as "violence" in Matthew and "force" in Luke, somewhat arbitrarily. Josephus uses the same word to refer to rape in his recounting of Amnon raping his sister Tamar in the book of 2 Samuel chapter 13. In any case, it is clear that Jesus foresaw that the Kingdom Movement will incite violence, even if the movement itself would be the victim of this violence and not the perpetrator. It is unlikely that this saying would be written by the early Christian community, as persecution of Christians was not widespread by this point, and certainly not in Palestine.

It is highly unlikely that Jesus specifically planned for his followers to take up arms like the Zealots eventually did, on the basis of there being very little evidence for this. On the other hand, there seems to have been a recognition that what he was doing would eventually lead to violence. The question must become: Did Jesus actually conceive of nonviolence as an active part of the kingdom? Was it an integral, or incidental, part of it?

Nonviolent resistance did exist among the Jews in Jesus's time, but it was always in *response* to a specific act of injustice. For example, Josephus reports in book 18, chapter 3 of *Antiquities*[6] that a multitude of Jews protested for days when Pilate displayed graven images of the emperor in Jerusalem. When Pilate ordered them to disperse or be killed, "they threw themselves upon the ground, and laid their necks bare, and said they would take their death very willingly, rather than the wisdom of their laws should be transgressed." Pilate backed down.

Total pacifism as an active strategy for change, like that conceived by Gandhi or Martin Luther King Jr., does not seem to have existed as an ongoing mass movement in the time of Jesus. Even the nonviolent Essenes were permitted to carry small hatchets to defend themselves from robbers and looked forward to a coming apocalyptic war. It is theoretically possible that Jesus created such a movement; however I do not see that in the text. What I see is an *incidental* nonviolence; a recognition that armed revolt

---

6. The same chapter, incidentally, where he mentions Jesus.

would end in destruction and failure and was not the correct way to bring about the kingdom of God.

I leave it open whether or not this was intended for all time. I can very easily conceive of a situation where Jesus did believe that eventually, when enough of the lost sheep of the house of Israel had joined his cause, violence would be necessary to displace the wicked powers of the Herodians, the temple, and Rome. The Kingdom Movement's primary mission of itinerant preachers and exorcists creating a prefigurative dual power community certainly involved some kind of culmination. I do not think Jesus was foolish enough to believe that eventually everyone would willingly join him and the transition would happen peacefully; his message was too exclusive to the lower classes, and his words for his enemies too harsh, for that to have been the case. The most likely scenario, in my opinion, is that he believed that cataclysmic wars were coming in the near future that would sweep away the ruling classes and leave the Kingdom Movement as the only legitimate power left, but that it was not necessarily the duty of the Kingdom Movement to wage these wars. I am utterly aware how tentative this suggestion must remain, for now, but for reasons that will soon become clear, I do not see a deliberate and integral pacifism in any of Jesus's teachings.

What is inarguable, however, is that violent revolution was not on the immediate agenda for the Kingdom Movement. So how, then, do we make sense of sayings like "turn the other cheek" and "do not resist evil" and "love your enemy"? That is the starting point for the next section.

RULES OF BEHAVIOR

This next complex of sayings, mostly from Q and preserved in the Sermon on the Mount but also in other sources, deals with behavior and discipline. They are among some of Jesus's best-known sayings, but have unfortunately been completely misinterpreted by all manner of Christians throughout the centuries.

The historical Jesus did not intend to replace or supersede Mosaic law, nor did he intend to found a new religion separate from Judaism. His ethical instructions were not universal precepts for how to be "Christly" as most Christians believe. They were instructions for how members of the Kingdom Movement should behave when interacting with each other, with outsiders, and with the authorities.

Matthew frames the Sermon on the Mount as a prophetic echo of Moses giving the original law on Mount Sinai, in line with his tendency to frame Jesus as a new Moses (compare Matthew's birth narrative with that for Moses in the exodus, for example). Even given Matthew's Christological agenda, however, this isn't entirely inappropriate. Jesus says in Q (Matt 5:18 = Luke 16:17):

> *For truly I tell you, until heaven and earth pass away, not one iota, not one stroke [κεραία], will pass from the law until all is accomplished.* (Matthew)

> *But it is easier for heaven and earth to pass away, than for one stroke [κεραίαν] in the law to be dropped.* (Luke)

The Greek word *keraia* (*keraian* in Luke) is probably a rough translation of a metaphor Jesus used for a tiny element of something, which Matthew embellished as "iota" (the smallest letter in the Greek alphabet). It has often been thought to represent a Hebrew scribal mark, but these were not in wide use during the time of Jesus and in any case Jesus was almost certainly illiterate like the vast majority of first-century Galilean Jews (and ancient people in general) and would not have used a word like that. Nor would he have used a Greek letter. Whatever Aramaic idiom stands behind this saying, however, in essence it does go back to the historical Jesus: he saw the kingdom as a fulfillment, not replacement, of the Mosaic Covenant. That even the Gentile Luke, a disciple of Paul (who represented the faction of Christians wanting to dispose of Mosaic law), transmitted this saying, is meaningful.

Yet this does not mean that Jesus, or any Jews for that matter, were blind slaves to the minutia of a centuries-old legal code. For one, the vast majority of people were illiterate and only knew the torah orally. More importantly, as we have seen with the Pharisees, the Mosaic law could be interpreted in various ways and supplemented or clarified by oral teachings. This is why Rabbinic Judaism has the Talmud, which is a collection of oral teachings literally called the "Oral Torah" and originating among the Pharisees and their ideological descendants.

So bear in mind as we consider a complex of sayings related to Mosaic law that they were not meant to be supersessionist. Jesus was not disputing or dispelling with, but rather *interpreting*, Mosaic law. These are often called the Six Antitheses, a dreadful misnomer if there ever was one. I will not reproduce them in their entirety here to save space; they are found in Matthew 5:21–47. They all follow a general pattern: Jesus introduces a theme, states the traditional Mosaic commandment on that theme ("You have heard it was said...") and then *intensifies* that commandment ("But I say to you...").

Murder is first, and of course the original teaching is "do not murder." Jesus goes even further, however, attacking the root cause of murder which is anger. Matthew sees this as the "fulfillment" of the law, and has Jesus say so, but it is important that these commands are seen as applying specifically within the context of the Kingdom Movement. Consider the next section of this "antithesis":

> *If you are angry with a brother or sister, you will be liable to judgment; and if you insult a brother or sister, you will be liable to the council; and if you say, "You fool," you will be liable to damnation. So when you are offering your gift at the altar, if you remember that your brother or sister has something against you, leave your gift there before the altar and go; first be reconciled to your brother or sister, and then come and offer your gift. Come to terms quickly with your accuser.* (Matt 5:22–25)

Here is a side-dig at those who obey the letter of the law (offering a gift at the altar) without keeping to the spirit (purging hate and anger from oneself). Compare it again with this excerpt from instructions Mao Zedong gave to committee leaders of the Communist Party during the Chinese Civil War:

> *Place problems on the table.... Do not talk behind people's backs. Whenever problems arise, call a meeting, place the problems on the table for discussion, take some decisions and the problems will be solved. If problems exist and are not placed on the table, they will remain unsolved for a long time and even drag on for years. ... Nothing is more important than mutual understanding, support and friendship.*[7]

Jesus's instructions here must be understood in the same context as Mao's. They served as a code of conduct or manual of discipline for how members of the Kingdom Movement were to act. They also served a prefigurative function, as Jesus sums up these instructions with "Therefore be perfect, as your heavenly Father is perfect" (Matthew) or "Be compassionate, as your Father is compassionate" (Luke) recalling "You shall be holy, for I the Lord your God am holy" (Lev 19:2).

7. Mao Zedong, *Methods of Work of Party Committees*, March 13, 1949.

So the next of the "antitheses" (I only use that name, and in quotation marks, for convenience's sake) concerns adultery, which again is forbidden in the Mosaic Covenant. A real antithesis would be the permission of adultery or forbidding of marriage; instead Jesus equates lust with adultery. Again, he targets the underlying feeling or emotion which leads to the bad behavior. After this Jesus also forbids divorce (saying that Moses only allowed it due to the "hardness of men's hearts"), which will be considered further in the next section on family.

The final three "antitheses" are oaths, retaliation, and love. Oaths is straightforward; members of the kingdom are not to swear oaths but to simply have their word be their word. It was a model of behavior and discipline that was meant to set members of the Kingdom Movement apart, to display their humility and trustworthiness to the people they ministered to.

Retaliation is a fascinating case. As many have pointed out before me, the original commandment—"an eye for an eye and a tooth for a tooth"—from Exodus 21:24 and Leviticus 24:20 was meant to call for *reciprocal retaliation*, despite later anti-Semitic Christian polemics against Judaism as a brutal or overly punitive religion. Its purpose was to *limit* retaliation so that the punishment did not exceed the crime.

Jesus's elaboration is different than his previous ones. *"Do not resist an evildoer,"* he says in Matthew 5:39. *"But if anyone strikes you on the right cheek, turn the other also; and if anyone wants to sue you and take your coat, give your cloak as well; and if anyone forces you to go one mile, go also the second mile. Give to everyone who begs from you, and do not refuse anyone who wants to borrow from you."*

Here again, at first glance, is the peace-loving hippie Jesus that so many progressive and liberal Christians love. First, at the beginning, the word translated as "resist"—*antistenai* (root: *anthistemi*) can have connotations of military opposition. In this case it plausibly means "do not violently resist" an evildoer, although ancient Jews probably did not have the same understanding of violent versus nonviolent resistance that we do today. In any case, "do not resist" does not mean "passively accept" as the next grouping of instructions makes clear.

The best explanation of these instructions in their own context comes from Walter Wink.[8] The key to this understanding is that the commandment limiting retaliation only applies to equals—certainly a slave does not

---

8. Wink, *Engaging the Powers*.

have the right to retaliate against his master (see, e.g., Exod 21:24–27 for this double standard in action).

Jesus's commandments about turning the other cheek, giving away your cloak, and going the extra mile are all intended to force your opponent, the "evildoer," to treat you as an equal. The right cheek is specified because to strike someone on the right cheek would require a backhand slap with the right hand (the left hand was only used for "unclean" tasks, for example it was prohibited to even gesture with this hand in Qumran's Community Rule).

> *A backhand slap was the usual way of admonishing inferiors. Masters backhanded slaves; husbands, wives; parents, children; men, women; Romans, Jews. We have here a set of unequal relations, in each of which retaliation would invite retribution. The only normal response would be cowering submission.*[9]

By turning the other cheek, the victim is forcing the oppressor to acknowledge them as an equal in humanity.

So it is also for the cloak; these outer garments were often used as collateral by debtors who had nothing else to offer. Mosaic law dictated that when this happened, the garments were to be returned in the evening, because the debtor might need it to sleep (Exod 22:25–27; Deut 24:10–13). By giving away the undergarment as well as the overcoat, the victim is publicly shaming their oppressor through their nakedness.

And finally, going the extra mile is a reference to Roman *angaria* laws, which had in various forms been widespread throughout the classical world since the time of the Persian Empire. The Roman law permitted legionaries to forcibly enlist peasants and citizens to carry their burdens for up to one mile for them. By going the extra mile, the victims of this cruel system of short-term slavery could take control of the situation and even force the legionaries to break the Roman laws, in effect discouraging this practice.

Finally, the commandment to give freely to beggars is very straightforward: members of the Kingdom Movement were servants, after all, and so sharing whatever they had with the less fortunate could have gone without saying.

This remarkable instruction shows the creative brilliance of Jesus's eschatological theory. Even within a movement not premised around building an army for insurrection, the Kingdom Movement found ways

---

9. Wink, *Engaging the Powers*, 176.

to subvert and even directly challenge the conventions of inequality in the current world.

This culminates with the final "antithesis," love. The Mosaic law commands love for one's neighbor (remember above, Jesus's addition about "hating one's enemy" is a characteristic contradiction meant to emphasize the former saying and not actually found in the Torah), but here Jesus commands love for one's enemies as well. There is an ill-fitting dig at tax collectors here that does not go back to the historical Jesus (he accepted the publicans, as many other pericopes make clear), but the essence of the teaching is that it is easy to love those who already love you, but love for one's enemies is much more difficult. The final line in chapter five is a summation of all we have seen: "Therefore be perfect, as your heavenly Father is perfect" (Matt 5:48). Members of the Kingdom Movement were, quite literally, representing God on Earth, and so they had to embody all of God's virtues (seen as justice, fairness, moral character, and equality) to the highest degree.

Other instructions emphasize moral perfection. *"If your hand causes you to stumble, cut it off . . . if your foot causes you to stumble, cut it off. . . . And if your eye causes you to stumble, tear it out; it is better for you to enter the kingdom of God with one eye than to have two eyes and be thrown into Gehenna"* (Mark 9:43–47; par. Matt 5 and Matt 18). Reminiscent of the commandment to "remove the log from your own eye" in Matthew 7:3–5, here we have another parallel with the revolutionary discipline of the Chinese Communists as instructed by Mao. It is linked again with servitude.

> *All our cadres, whatever their rank, are servants of the people, and whatever we do is to serve the people. How then can we be reluctant to discard any of our bad traits?*[10]

For Jesus, true servitude requires absolutely impeccable moral character. Yet members of the kingdom are not expected to come already morally perfect; they are expected to struggle within themselves and with their comrades to discard their own bad traits.

These themes continue throughout the Sermon on the Mount. Members are not to give for the sake of being seen (Matt 6:2–4). They are to pray privately, emphasizing their humility (Matt 7–13 = Luke 11:1–4). This prayer, often called the Lord's Prayer, entreats God for remission of debt/sins (it should be understood as both, as debt is a common theme in Jesus's

---

10. From a speech given on December 15, 1944.

teachings and parables but was also a common Aramaic metaphor for sin) as well as "daily bread," signifying the material needs of the people to whom the kingdom belonged.

Members of the kingdom were instructed not to collect material wealth (Matt 6:19), for they could not serve both God and money (6:24). They were supposed to trust in God, and implicitly in the people they ministered to, for their material needs (Matt 6:25–34), recalling *the Mission* and the interrelationship between proclaiming the kingdom and sharing meals. They were told not to judge others, and to see to their own negative traits before criticizing each other's (Matt 7:1–5 = Luke 6:37–38).

These laid the basis for later teachings, such as that found in Matthew 18:15–20, which presumes settled churches and so traces to the early Christian community and not the lifetime of Jesus. However, one can see the continuity between this teaching and Jesus's, and how it was adapted from his ethical instructions to serve as a guideline for how members of a Christian church should act.

> *If another member of the church sins against you, go and point out the fault when the two of you are alone. If the member listens to you, you have regained that one. But if you are not listened to, take one or two others along with you, so that every word may be confirmed by the evidence of two or three witnesses. If the member refuses to listen to them, tell it to the church; and if the offender refuses to listen even to the church, let such a one be to you as a Gentile and a tax collector.*

The misunderstanding of Jesus's ethical teachings as universal precepts for living in the twentieth or twenty-first centuries is one of the greatest corruptions of the gospel perpetrated by modern Christianity. These teachings are many things: they are radical, even revolutionary; they are subversive and creative solutions to problems faced by the poor and marginalized in first-century Palestine; they are valuable and worth studying and applying in modern times. What they are *not*, however, is universal, nor are they banal or individualistic. They presume a revolutionary community dedicated to the realization of the kingdom of God, a place of unbrokered equality and justice for the poor, hungry, and outcast. That is the context Jesus taught them in, and that is the context they must be practiced in, if they are to be practiced at all.

THEORY

THE DESTRUCTION OF THE FAMILY

This is one of the more challenging teachings of Jesus, because family as a concept is still viewed very positively by our culture. Yet Jesus's statements about the family are almost uniformly negative, even scathing. We will examine the complex of sayings, then delve into their social context.

The first double-attested saying comes from Mark 3:33–35 (copied in Matt 12:48–50 and Luke 8:21), with a parallel in saying 99 of *Thomas*.

> *Then his mother and his brothers came; and standing outside, they sent to him and called him. A crowd was sitting around him; and they said to him, "Your mother and your brothers and sisters are outside, asking for you." And he replied, "Who are my mother and my brothers?" And looking at those who sat around him, he said, "Here are my mother and my brothers! Whoever does the will of God is my brother and sister and mother."* (Mark)

The next comes from both Q (Matt 10:37 = Luke 14:26) and *Thomas* 55. Luke and *Thomas* agree against Matthew's wording:

> *Whoever comes to me and does not hate father and mother, wife and children, brothers and sisters, yes, and even life itself, cannot be my disciple. Whoever does not carry the cross and follow me cannot be my disciple.* (Luke)

These examples are crucial because they show a critique of the family in three independent and early sources, Mark, Q, and *Thomas*. The former saying is particularly instructive, because it contradicts a later historical fact that we know from Paul and Josephus: that at least one of Jesus's brothers (and probably more of his family), James the Just, was actually an important leader in the very early church and possibly within the pre-Easter Kingdom Movement itself. Indeed, Acts also reports that Mary, Jesus's mother, and his brothers were there from Jesus's ascension at the very latest (Acts 1:14).

What is probable is that Jesus, as the oldest man in his family (remember Joseph is out of the picture by this point and Jesus could never have plausibly been given a virgin birth origin if he'd had an older sibling) inspired division within his own family when he left the carpenter's trade to follow John and eventually begin his own ministry. The eldest male in a family was the head of household, responsible for the well-being of all the rest of them, and Jesus leaving to join John the Baptist and eventually found his own movement could have been seen as an abdication of that responsibility.

Eventually, however, as the Kingdom Movement grew, Jesus's family came to believe in what he was doing and joined it. There is no direct evidence for this, of course, but it is the simplest and likeliest explanation for the contradiction between tension within Jesus's own family (see also Mark 3:21; 6:1–6) and their eventual positions as leaders or respected members of the early Christian community.

The aforementioned "not peace, but a sword" saying, from Q and *Thomas*, belongs here too. This time Matthew and *Thomas* agree against Luke, who changes "sword" to "division," the literal meaning. Here is Matthew's version:

> *Do not think that I have come to bring peace to the earth; I have not come to bring peace, but a sword. For I have come to set a man against his father, and a daughter against her mother, and a daughter-in-law against her mother-in-law; and one's foes will be members of one's own household.* (Matt 10:34–36; Luke 12:49–53; *Thomas* 16)

Q's saying includes references to daughters, mothers, daughters-in-law, and mothers-in-law, while *Thomas* only specifies fathers against sons. Q's version is closer to the original; the final redactors of *Thomas* were misogynists (adding the grossly sexist final saying, 114, which was not part of the original text and has nothing to do with the historical Jesus) and the specification of daughters and mothers "in-law" is too specific to have been an accident.

Jesus explicitly tells us that the coming of the kingdom will tear families and households apart, specifically along generational lines. What is at play here? The traditional Christian reading is that one must be ready to put commitment to Christ above one's family ties, but this is surface-level and still in tension with the traditional view of the Christian community itself as a "family"; with the husband as householder and head-of-family over the wife as homemaker and bearer-of-children and children at the bottom of the pyramid mimicking Christ-as-bridegroom and church-as-bride, with the laity as the children at the bottom.

Indeed, Jesus often spoke of God as a "father" so there is obviously more going on here. We will begin with a materialist understanding of the family itself.

The first note of import is that while the "traditional family" of Jesus's time looked different than the nuclear family of conservative America, the role it played in society was similar. In the Roman-Jewish-Mediterranean world of first-century Palestine, the extended family was the smallest unit of society, just as conservative Christianity views the nuclear family (as opposed to the individual) as the building block of American society.

The head of the Mediterranean family unit was the *paterfamilias*, usually the elder male of the family and often the grandfather. His male children and their male children worked to support the family, while daughters were married off to other families (other daughters, of course, married *into* their family). Extended families often lived together, working their ancestral land and providing for the family's name over generations.

That was the ideal situation. Jesus's experience, however was different. His class upbringing must be considered before any examination of his views on the family, because as Friedrich Engels has taught us:

> *The determining factor in history is, in the final instance, the production and reproduction of the immediate essentials of life. . . . On the one side, the production of the means of existence, of articles of food and clothing, dwellings, and of the tools necessary for that production; on the other side, the production of human beings themselves, the propagation of the species. The social organization under which the people of a particular historical epoch and a particular country live is determined by both kinds of production: by the stage of development of labor on the one hand and of the family on the other.*[11]

So the ways in which humans propagate are inextricably and dialectically linked to material conditions. We must not make the mistake of thinking of the family as some static, biological institution that has endured for millennia. It is a social institution that has evolved in numerous ways throughout human history, and kinship and family is one of the most important aspects of cultural anthropology, even called "the basic discipline of the subject" by anthropologist Robin Fox.[12] Yet this discipline has been overwhelmingly stifled by two related limitations: Eurocentrism, and bourgeois ideology, as shown definitively by Chris Knight.[13] According to Knight (drawing on Fox and others), bourgeois European anthropologists have interpreted data about indigenous systems of human kinship within the paradigm of individualistic, Western conceptions of the family, resulting in an abject failure to see the family as an evolving social institution.

---

11. Engels, *Origin of the Family*, 35.
12. Fox, *Kinship and Marriage*, 10.
13. Knight, "Early Human Kinship."

This is partially in reaction to Engels's book that I just quoted, as well as the work of his predecessor, Lewis Morgan. The fact that Engels was a communist and his work became "state doctrine" of the Soviet Union gave bourgeois Western scholars the impetus to discredit it by any means necessary, leading to astonishing levels of academic dishonesty throughout the work of twentieth-century anthropologists. "Once Engels had incorporated Morgan's findings into the socialist canon, however, no one could write neutrally on such topics any more," Knight writes. "Once Engels had endorsed it, Morgan's theory was destined to become a casualty of the central conflict of the age [the Cold War]."

We can no longer afford to make that mistake. We must embrace historical materialism, for its discoveries have been borne out by science. The primary thesis of *Origin of the Family* is that human kinship (the ways we understand our relationships with parents, siblings, grandparents, cousins, etc.) evolves and changes based on material conditions. Morgan and Engels (among other social scientists at the time) reductively categorized human societies to three "stages"—savagery, barbarism, and civilization. These were not meant to be chauvinistic, but of course have become so over time and are no longer used, and it is now recognized that a "three-stage" evolution of human society culminating in "civilization" is irredeemably simplistic and Eurocentric (although it's debatable whether European civilization was meant to be normative for this stage; the first "civilization" to fall in this category would be Sumeria, in modern Iraq).

Be that as it may, Knight and others[14] have shown that the primary element from which Engels drew all his other conclusions is true. In prehistoric hunter-gatherer societies where there is no concept of private property, the family simply does not exist. As peoples move to horticultural societies, amassing surpluses of food and settling permanently or semi-permanently, early forms of family begin to coalesce. The earliest forms of the family are matrilineal, with kinship reckoned by the *mother's* line. It is only when/if a society develops agriculture and/or animal husbandry, leading to massive surpluses of private property that must be kept within the *gens* (extended tribal family, similar to "clan") that the family begins to narrow and focus on patrilineality. This is where monogamy springs into existence, as ensuring a woman has only one sexual partner (her husband) is the only way in a pre-modern society to absolutely ensure that her children really are her husband's.

---

14. Opie and Power, "Grandmothering and Female Coalitions."

Elements of these earlier forms of the family remain evident in language and customs long after they have passed out of common practice. We need look no further than the Hebrew Bible:

> When brothers reside together, and one of them dies and has no son, the wife of the deceased shall not be married outside the family to a stranger. Her husband's brother shall go in to her, taking her in marriage, and performing the duty of a husband's brother to her. (Deut 25:5)

This so-called Levirate Marriage is the remnant of a form of sibling group marriage, prevalent in many societies (arguably in *every* society at a certain stage in its prehistory) that have not yet reached what Morgan and Engels would have called "civilization." In this loose family formation, marriage is not an ironclad bond between two individuals but rather two groups of siblings who are to some degree sexually available to each other. It is not sexist; women may mate with their husbands' brothers as freely as men with their wife's sisters. Even calling it "marriage" feels wrong, because the cultural idea of marriage as a union of only two people is so ingrained, but this was a formalized institution.

But the institution of marriage narrows and turns patriarchal the more a society becomes based on private property and its heritability. Finally we end with the individual family, "freed" from obligations to the larger clan or tribe, and here, as Marx and Engels write in *The German Ideology*, is where exploitation becomes widespread: "*The unequal distribution . . . of [labor] and its products . . . the nucleus, the first form, of which lies in the family, where wife and children are the slaves of the husband.*"[15]

This is why Jesus opposed the family. Because it is by its nature a hierarchical and patriarchal institution based on private property, it had no place in the kingdom of God. His own family, whether they supported him or not, had nothing to do with it. His blistering criticism of family is, like the open commensality that characterized the main practice of the Kingdom Movement, an attack on the fundamental inequality of class society, and the honor-shame mores of the Greco-Roman world.

But Jesus did not just attack the patriarchal and authoritarian family—he also conceived of the kingdom as a new type of family, in which only God was the Father. Jesus, radical as he was, stopped short of challenging God's maleness, but his calling God "father" does not mean that

---

15. Marx and Engels, *German Ideology*, 51–52.

the kingdom was meant to be male-dominated. The father as the head of family was responsible for the well-being of all of the members of that family; and the evidence makes the absolute equality of all members clear, men and women alike. So there were women apostles during and presumably before the lifetime of Paul,[16] and a teaching found quite independently in Paul and *Thomas* specifies that, to enter the kingdom you must *"make the male and the female one and the same, so that the male not be male nor the female female"* (*Thomas* 22) and *"there is no longer male and female; for all of you are one in Christ Jesus"* (Gal 3:28). Furthermore, John Dominic Crossan has argued strongly that the itinerant prophesying described in *the Mission* could very well have included women prophets.[17]

So Jesus was using a motif his audience would understand—God as Father—to illustrate the new, radically universal familyhood within the kingdom of God. Even the word kingdom—*basileus* in Greek—was chosen intentionally to contrast the Kingdom Movement with the Roman Empire, which thought of itself as a kingdom ("empire" is a later term that historians use to differentiate it from the Roman Monarchy in the 8th through 6th centuries BCE). The use of overwhelmingly male language is an archaism that may well be better off abandoned—I have used "kingdom" throughout this book out of convenience and simplicity, but the principle of dynamic equivalence suggests that better terms might be God as "householder" or "caretaker," and kingdom as "realm" or "community."

The family is the greatest example of Jesus's teachings and how they cannot be properly understood without historical materialism. The true genius of Jesus was that, like many of the Hebrew prophets before him, he recognized the evils and injustices of class society within institutions such as the family or conventions such as honor/shame and clean/unclean.

This dramatic and ruthless critique of the established order and the proclamation of its impending supplantation by a revolutionary and radical new type of world, a world where the poor and marginalized would lead and the wealthy would be cast down, could not help but bring Jesus into conflict with the authorities, even if he did try to keep it nonviolent. We know now what Jesus did, and what he taught. We understand his goals and, if we also long for liberation from oppression and total justice, we even sympathize with him.

---

16. Most notably Junia and Priscilla.
17. Crossan, *Historical Jesus*, 334–35.

THEORY

Now we turn to the inevitable conclusion of such a quixotic mission. We will look at how Jesus's ministry, and his life, ended, a fate which is no less tragic for how predictable it is. We will see that the powers of oppression and injustice reacted to Jesus the same way they have reacted to revolutionaries throughout history: with brutal, uncompromising violence.

Chapter 5

PASSION

He commanded them to set up a cross, as if he were going to hang Eleazar upon it immediately. The sight of this occasioned a sore grief among those that were in the citadel: and they groaned vehemently; and cried out that they could not bear to see him thus destroyed. Whereupon Eleazar besought them not to disregard him, now he was going to suffer the most wretched death; and exhorted them to save themselves, by yielding to the Roman power, and good fortune: since all other people were now conquered by them.
— Josephus, Jewish War, book VII, ch. 6

AN IGNOBLE END

That Jesus was crucified has been shown to be one of the most reliable facts about him that we can know. It is attested not only in the gospels and Paul, but also by our best non-Christian source, Josephus, who found the information credible enough to include. Finally, it is perhaps the most solid example of the criterion of embarrassment at work: the idea of a crucified Messiah was so outrageous that nobody would have invented it. Paul admits that it is "foolishness" and "a stumbling block" to the unconverted in 1 Corinthians 1:18, 23, and Justin Martyr in the second century says that non-Christians see the belief in a crucified Messiah as "madness."[1]

It also tells us something else about the historical Jesus, something which given all we have analyzed thus far should not be surprising: Jesus was considered a threat to the established order of society, for the purpose of crucifixion was dissuasion.

Consider Eleazar, referenced in the quote above. He was a Zealot rebel leader in the war against the Romans who was captured and set to be crucified, suffering "the most wretched death" according to Josephus. He was so popular and the punishment so cruel that the Jews surrendered the fortress of Machaerus, which had been Antipas's home, without a struggle, rather than let him suffer this fate.

It is difficult in our Christianized world to imagine crucifixion apart from Jesus, but we must try so that we may understand how it was that Jesus was crucified rather than hung, beheaded, stoned, burnt alive, drawn and quartered, or executed by some other measure. Crucifixion was uniquely awful for reasons that it is difficult for a modern person to empathize with.

The seminal study of crucifixion is Martin Hengel's *Crucifixion*,[2] although Hengel does not devote enough attention to Jewish views of crucifixion. For that we will rely on the work of David W. Chapman.[3]

Hengel devotes a whole chapter to emphasizing the unusual cruelty of the cross, not only by our modern standards but even by the standards of the ancient world. In the Roman period it always involved torture and beatings beforehand (which we see in the account of Jesus) and was often done in a mass fashion, to large groups of rebels or slaves (Josephus gives several accounts of this happening in his books). It was so horrible, in fact, that it seems to have bordered on a taboo subject among the Romans:

> *It is certainly the case that the Roman world was largely unanimous that crucifixion was a horrific, disgusting business. There is therefore hardly any mention of it in inscriptions. . . . Crucifixion was widespread and frequent, above all in Roman times, but the cultured literary world wanted to have nothing to do with it, and as a rule kept quiet about it.*[4]

---

1. *First Apology*, ch. 13.
2. Hengel, *Crucifixion*.
3. Chapman, *Perceptions on Crucifixion*.
4. Hengel, *Crucifixion*, 37–38.

Hengel reports that crucifixion was a crime with an important class component. "Because of its harshness, crucifixion was almost always inflicted only on the lower class; the upper class could reckon with more 'humane' punishment. Here we have a real case of 'class justice.'"[5]

Later he writes of the political goals that the Romans (and others) achieved through crucifixion:

> *Crucifixion was already, as in Rome, the punishment for serious crimes against the state and for high treason among the Persians, to some degree in Greece and above all among the Carthaginians. That is, it was a religious-political punishment, with the emphasis falling on the political side; however, the two aspects cannot yet be separated in the ancient world. . . . Crucifixion was also a means of waging war and securing peace, of wearing down rebellious cities under siege, of breaking the will of conquered peoples.*[6]

Finally, Hengel emphasizes that a part of the horror of crucifixion was that the crucified victim could rarely expect a burial in a world that believed proper burial was crucial to a proper afterlife. So, for example, ancient writers mention crucified victims left as "evil food for birds of prey and grim pickings for dogs."[7]

> *Crucifixion was aggravated further by the fact that quite often its victims were never buried. It was a stereotyped picture that the crucified victim served as food for wild beasts and birds of prey. In this way his humiliation was made complete. What it meant for a man in antiquity to be refused burial, and the dishonor which went with it, can hardly be appreciated by modern man.*[8]

It is instructive here that of all the thousands of crucifixions attested in the ancient world, only one or possibly two skeletons of crucified individuals have ever been found *in the entire world*.[9] This confirms Hengel's assertion that these people were only offered burial in extremely rare cases.

5. Hengel, *Crucifixion*, 34.
6. Hengel, *Crucifixion*, 46, emphasis added.
7. Pseudo-Manetho, quoted in Hengel, *Crucifixion*, 9.
8. Hengel, *Crucifixion*, 87–88.
9. The first and definite case was of a first-century Jew named Yehohanan, from Jerusalem, whose remains were found in an ossuary in a family tomb (a sign that his family was relatively well-off). The second possible case was discovered in 2007 in Italy, but it was not until an April 2018 article in *Archaeological and Anthropological Sciences* that examiners postulated the body may have been of a crucified slave, based on a hole in the heel.

PASSION

Chapman's study of crucifixion in Jewish thought and literature is the necessary complement to Hengel's work.[10] He emphasizes a few key points. First,

> the Crucified Brigand was a common figure in Judaea and Galilee in the late Second Temple period. Josephus frequently testifies to brigandage in this period, also mentioning an instance of mass crucifixion of brigands. Roman policy, not limited to Judaea, often called for the crucifixion of such brigands. Such an empire-wide policy likely led to a common association of the cross with brigands and rebels.[11]

Note that the word "brigand" (*lestai* in Greek; what the men crucified next to Jesus are described as) does not mean a simple thief or highway robber. It is an explicitly political term for a rebel who uses banditry as a tactic.[12]

Deuteronomy 21:22–23 contains a proscription of allowing bodies of those executed and "hung on a tree" to remain there all night; they must be buried before nightfall because those hung on a tree are "under God's curse." Jews were divided on whether or not this applied to death by crucifixion, according to Chapman (216), but Paul quotes the Scripture in relation to Jesus in Galatians 3:13, so it is appropriate to consider it.

This curse had varying understandings, but Hengel notes, "The earliest extant view . . . is that the hung person is cursed by God."[13] This is certainly how Paul understands it, although he interprets it through his idea that the sacrifice of Jesus on the cross set the stage for the supersession of the Mosaic law.

We are focusing so heavily on crucifixion because it is indisputably the firmest ground we have to stand on when talking about the death of Jesus. The rest of the Passion Narrative, as we shall soon see, is incredibly problematic from a historical perspective, as is the following resurrection. But here we can be sure what we are dealing with. Jesus, as magnificent a teacher and prophet and revolutionary as he was, met the same ignoble end as thousands of others before and after him. It was unimaginably painful, yes, but also so psychologically cruel and socially terrifying that it made it impossible for most Jews to accept that Jesus could have been any kind

---

10. Hengel even bemoaned that a more thorough study into specifically Jewish attitudes toward crucifixion is necessary.
11. Chapman, *Perceptions on Crucifixion*, 213.
12. See Grunewald, *Bandits in the Roman Empire*.
13. Chapman, *Perceptions on Crucifixion*, 148.

of Messiah. He was, like all the other bandits and prophets and rebellious slaves condemned to the cross, a lowly man who got big ideas about changing the world, and so the state made an example of him.

It is uncomfortable, even distressing, that such a brutal and shameful fate befell a man that Christians naturally want to exalt. I do not wish to glorify or romanticize the suffering of crucifixion, as many Christians do. I do not interpret it through the later Christian lens of atonement theology, whereby Jesus suffered on the cross to earn forgiveness for the sins of humankind. The historical Jesus said and did nothing of the sort.

What I see in crucifixion is the macabre violence to which the powers of this world will resort to maintain their privileged status. I see the heart-rending, but not unexpected, death of any person brave (or foolish) enough to challenge the ruling class. I see the struggle of millions of other prophets and rebels and dreamers and freedom-fighters since the beginning of the dawn of class society who met the same fate fighting for a world in which everyone is free and equal.

THE PASSION

Leading up to the crucifixion, of course, is an entire narrative of Jesus's last week, which he spends in Jerusalem (in Judea, not Galilee), known as the passion. There are numerous historical issues at play here.

The first and foremost is that the entire Passion Narrative is known to us only by a single source. Mark's narrative, in chapters 11–16, forms the basis for Matthew's, Luke's, and probably John's Passion Narratives (although Matthew and Luke variously intersperse some Q material throughout). Whether Mark wrote it himself or copied it from an earlier source is irrelevant; Q says nothing of it, nor does *Thomas* or the *Didache* or Paul (aside from a few general agreements).

These do not necessarily mean that Mark created it out of whole cloth. Obviously the crucifixion really happened, so at least that one detail can be given to the historical Jesus, and perhaps others. But we are no longer dealing with collections of pericopes or sayings organized according to the theological or textual or apologetic aims of each individual Evangelist: we are dealing with a single narrative, essentially one very long pericope, with dozens of subsections.

Next, there is a problem that I have already alluded to with the story of Barabbas, the rebel who Pilate pardoned for the Jewish crowd in Mark

15:6–15. This story cannot possibly be historical. It flies in the face of everything we know about Pilate from Josephus; it relies on a supposed legal practice (pardoning prisoners because of a religious festival) that simply did not and could not have existed; and it absolutely stinks of post-war polemics: the Jews chose the rebel Barabbas over the savior Jesus, which is why the Roman-Jewish war happened. This section, at least, cannot come from earlier than the year 70, and is likely a Markan creation (and points to a later date for the entire Passion Narrative).

Most of the material within this narrative is like this. One of the simplest examples comes at the very beginning of the Passion Narrative, the Triumphal Entry.

> *When they were approaching Jerusalem, at Bethpage and Bethany, near the Mount of Olives, he sent two of his disciples and said to them, "Go into the village ahead of you, and immediately as you enter it, you will find tied there a colt that has never been ridden; untie it and bring it. If anyone says to you, 'Why are you doing this?' just say this, 'The Lord needs it and will send it back here immediately.'" They went away and found a colt tied near a door, outside in the street. As they were untying it, some of the bystanders said to them, "What are you doing, untying the colt?" They told them what Jesus had said; and they allowed them to take it. Then they brought the colt to Jesus and threw their cloaks on it; and he sat on it. Many people spread their cloaks on the road, and others spread leafy branches that they had cut in the fields.* (Mark 11:1–8)

As Matthew's version in chapter 21 of his gospel makes explicit, this is a reference to Zechariah 9:9: *"Rejoice greatly, O daughter Zion! Shout aloud, O daughter Jerusalem! Lo, your king comes to you; triumphant and victorious is he, humble and riding on a donkey, on a colt, the foal of a donkey."*

It is possible, of course, that Jesus intentionally performed this action as a prophetic demonstration to recall Zechariah. The meaning of such an action would be clear to all those who saw it: Jesus would be essentially proclaiming himself the king of Israel.

Is this likely to have been something the historical Jesus would have done? Or does this fit better within a post-Easter context, when the earliest Christians had exalted Jesus to messiahship and near-divinity? Based on all the reconstruction we have done thus far, I think the latter much more likely. Jesus's movement was not primarily about himself, and such an action would fly in the face of that basic conclusion. What I see here is the beginning of a fiction, a parable expressing the belief of the early Christian community that Jesus was the king.

Consider the passage Luke puts right after the scene with the donkey, in 19:41–44. This speech is completely unique to Luke's gospel:

> As he came near and saw the city, he wept over it, saying, "If you, even you, had only recognized on this day the things that make for peace! But now they are hidden from your eyes. Indeed, the days will come upon you, when your enemies will set up ramparts around you and surround you, and hem you in on every side. They will crush you to the ground, you and your children within you, and they will not leave within you one stone upon another; because you did not recognize the time of your visitation from God."

The problems with this speech should be obvious by now. Here Luke is having Jesus lament over the future destruction of Jerusalem, and his interpretation of that event is, as we saw with the Barabbas story earlier, the failure of the Jews of Jerusalem to recognize Jesus as the Messiah. A much later historical and religious context has been put into the story of Jesus's entry to Jerusalem.

So it is for much of the Passion Narrative. Any good reconstruction of the historical Jesus, in my opinion, avails itself by sticking to a minimalist philosophy. That is, every saying, every deed, every event, is suspect unless there is good reason to believe otherwise. So we will focus first on the elements that I have good reason to believe *are* historical, rather than going piece-by-piece through the entire passion. Because the results are likely to be unsatisfying to most Christians, I will then proceed with a few examples where I feel it is important to illustrate why they are probably *not* historical. Finally, we will conclude with a general summary of the death of Jesus to put it all in context.

Passover

The sources state that Jesus and his disciples came to Jerusalem, far from the regular setting of the Kingdom Movement's activities, for the Pesach or Passover festival. This was the most important of all the Jewish festivals, with thousands of devout pilgrims thronging the city each year. According to Josephus, "*They observe it with enthusiasm, and it is their custom to slaughter sacrifices in greater number than at any other festival. An innumerable multitude of people come out of the country, and from abroad also, in order to worship God.*"[14]

Passover celebrates the deliverance of the Israelites from slavery in Egypt in the book of Exodus. Sacrifice is built into the festival, as it is based on the story in Exodus 11 of Yahweh killing the firstborn children and animals of all the Egyptians, but "passing over" the houses of the Israelites, who were instructed to mark their doors with lamb's blood. In memorial, a lamb, the "Paschal lamb," was sacrificed on the night before the holiday.

The Passover festival had a reputation for being a tinderbox atmosphere. Josephus records many disturbances taking place during it, including the execution of another miracle-worker named Onias or Honi the Circle-Drawer, who he describes as "a righteous man."[15] There are riots, conflicts between Roman soldiers and Jewish pilgrims, and protests by Samaritans. In such an atmosphere, the temple priests and Roman authorities were quick to hand down swift judgments and deal with troublemakers summarily and violently.

The question can be asked whether Jesus regularly attended Passover as all Jewish men were supposed to do. My answer is, probably not. He and other Jews who lived far from Jerusalem likely went every few years or as they were able, but not every single year unless they were of means. This does not mean it was his first time in Jerusalem, but only that it was most likely his first time there since the beginning of his ministry, which in my estimation lasted around two years.[16]

Against this backdrop, it seems possible that Jesus's execution could have taken place at Passover. While there may have been theological motivations in identifying Jesus with the Paschal Lamb as the sacrifice for the sins of humankind, it is just as easy to imagine the reverse process, a death at Passover later interpreted within a Paschal context. The idea of Jesus traveling to Passover, which was a dangerous atmosphere for rabble-rousers, and being executed easily passes the sniff test, so I see no reason to discount it.

To go further, however, we need is an inciting event. Entering the city with a crowd of people chanting that he was the King of Israel could have

---

14. *Antiquities*, XVII.9.
15. *Antiquities*, XIV.2.
16. All of the events in the synoptic account can fit within a one-year period, but there is no reason to think they had an accurate portrayal of elapsed time as a goal. I judge that his ministry would have needed at least two years to properly take hold, but probably no more than three.

been such an incident, but as stated I do not believe Jesus actually did that. The next incident, however, is much more probable.

The Cleansing of the Temple

> *And he entered the Temple and began to drive out those who were selling and those who were buying in the temple, and he overturned the tables of the money changers and the seats of those who sold doves; and he would not allow anyone to carry anything through the Temple. He was teaching and saying, "Is it not written, 'My house shall be called a house of prayer for all nations'? But you have made it a den of robbers." (Mark 11:15–17; Matt 21, Luke 19)*

There is a lot to unpack here. Most importantly, however, Mark's gospel portrays this as the event that led "the chief priests and the scribes" to decide that they needed to have this Jesus fellow killed once and for all.

This sounds believable, however I would question whether it was really the "chief priests" or any of the Jewish authorities who condemned Jesus to death, given the early Christians' obsession with putting as much blame for Jesus's crucifixion on the Jews as possible. Be that as it may, the idea of Jesus staging some kind of protest or direct action at the temple, in the charged atmosphere of Passover, and being arrested and executed for it is a very reasonable explanation for his death.

Another factor lending this credibility is that it has multiple attestation. John's version is in a completely different place in his gospel (near the beginning) and he gives it a wildly different scriptural-interpretive context. Next there is saying 71 of *Thomas*, which reads *"I will destroy this house, and no one will be able to build it."* April DeConick dates this saying to the original, independent and earliest layer of *Thomas*,[17] meaning it must be taken very seriously amid this background. *Thomas* does not refer to the temple directly, of course, but what else could it be referring to? That noun, house (*oikos* in Greek), is the link. We have here a saying from the very earliest layer of tradition about the destruction (which may be figurative or literal) of the temple.

Jesus's prophetic statement about the temple refers to Isaiah 56:7 and Jeremiah 7:11. In Jeremiah, which contains the "den of robbers" quote, Yahweh is condemning the temple authorities for oppressing *"the alien, the orphan, and the widow,"* and *"shed[ding] innocent blood in this place."*

---

17. DeConick, "Original Gospel of Thomas."

Yahweh ends his condemnation with the promise to utterly destroy *"the house [oikos in the Septuagint] that is called by my name"* (Jer 7:14).

Calling this act *the cleansing of the temple* is probably a misnomer. Those money-changers and merchants selling doves were not the source of the perversion or uncleanliness. Jesus probably did not like them, but his goal was not a "cleansing" of the temple by getting rid of them as if that was all that was required. The purpose of forcing them out was that it ground the sacrificial amenities of the temple to a halt. It would be more accurate to call this the *symbolic destruction* of the temple, as Jesus felt, in true prophetic fashion, that the temple had become a den of iniquity and oppression and foresaw its replacement or destruction. Since we know he created a dual-power alternative to it, this fits snugly with the rest of what he taught and believed.

Here is my best reconstruction of what happened based on the very scarce data. I do not think that Jesus came to the temple to "cleanse" it, nor do I think, as some have suggested, that he went to it simply to perform the proper rituals and then became enraged at the sight of money-changers. I think that he and some of his followers went there in order to stage a prophetic demonstration and gain followers among the Jerusalem crowd. They probably used some form of violence (John has Jesus fashioning a whip and beating people) to remove the authorities from the temple, but did not kill or seriously injure anybody as that would have immediately brought the soldiers down hard on them. Jesus's aim was to grab people's attention, prophesy against the temple just as Jeremiah had done, and escape into the crowd. I think that he had planned this for some time, and expected that like in Galilee and like in the case of John the Baptist before him, he would be protected by the masses who welcomed his message.

Obviously, it did not turn out that way. We will return to the question of why later, but for now we will move on to what I judge, believe it or not, to be the last two historical elements from the Passion Narrative, aside from the crucifixion itself.

Betrayal by Judas

I need not reproduce the relevant passages here; they do not differ enough to matter for the present reconstruction. But in 1 Corinthians 11:23–24 Paul does mention that Jesus was "betrayed" so I accept some historical basis. There is no more historical information whatsoever on Judas, other than in the first chapter of Acts where he is replaced among the Twelve, which I find dubious. I defer to Occam's Razor: Jesus was probably betrayed or identified after the temple ruckus by one of his disciples named Judas, but any information further than that is beyond our reach.

Peter's Denial

> *Peter said to him, "Even though all become deserters, I will not."*
> *Jesus said to him, "Truly I tell you, this day, this very night, before the cock crows twice, you will deny me three times." (Mark 14:29–30; Matt 26:33–34; Luke 22:34)*

Peter's three denials all appear later, in Mark 14:67–72.

Now obviously, in keeping with the ardently materialist and minimalist reconstructive method I'm using, I do not think that Jesus predicted any such denial. Nor do I think Peter's denials happened the way they are portrayed in the gospels, nor do I even presume that the "denials" were limited only to Peter. What I think is likely about this element is that Jesus's followers, after he was arrested, *did* deny and abandon him to save their own skins. One of them, Judas, even helped the authorities capture Jesus.

I base my judgment mostly on the criterion of embarrassment; I see no reason for the early Christians to invent this element out of nowhere, and they progressively take pains to rehabilitate Peter in the resurrection appearances as he was known as one of the founders of the church. A denial or abandonment of Jesus by his followers also fits neatly within my larger reconstruction of the death of Jesus, which relies on his followers having had little idea what happened to him after his arrest.

I expect that this brief four-element reconstruction (*Passover-temple-betrayal-denial*) might strike those familiar with the Passion Narrative as somewhat lean, even disappointingly so. So I will address a couple of well-known elements of the passion and why I do not believe they were historical occurrences.

The Last Supper and the Eucharist

The Last Supper as the basis for the Christian Eucharist is probably the most important ritual in all Christendom, so I understand this is fraught territory. However, I do not believe that the Eucharist was instituted by Jesus, nor do I believe the Last Supper actually happened.

First, the matter of sources. We do have two separate sources for the Last Supper, but their contradictions and the ways in which they are handled make it clear that they are tenuous. The first and best source is Paul, in 1 Corinthians 11:23–26:

> *The Lord Jesus on the night when he was betrayed took bread, and when he had given thanks, he broke it, and said, "This is my body which is for you. Do this in remembrance of me." In the same way also the cup, after supper, saying, "This cup is the new covenant in my blood. Do this, as often as you drink it, in remembrance of me." For as often as you eat this bread and drink this cup, you proclaim the Lord's death until he comes.*

Here now is Mark's version.

> *As they were eating, he took bread, and blessed, and broke it, and gave it to them, and said, "Take; this is my body." And he took a cup, and when he had given thanks he gave it to them, and they drank of it. And he said to them, "This is my blood of the covenant, which is poured out for many. Truly, I say to you, I shall not drink again of the fruit of the vine until that day when I shall drink it new in the kingdom of God." (Mark 14:22–25; Matt 26:26–29; Luke 22:15–20)*

Some differences are immediately apparent. Only the Markan formulation is identified explicitly with Passover (although Paul's is implicit). Paul specifies that the ritual is done in "remembrance" of Jesus (hold onto this fact) while the Markan formulation connects it with the coming kingdom and actually gives no obvious indication that this is meant as the institution of any kind of ritual. Reading Mark's version shorn of what we already know about the Eucharist from Christianity would leave one thinking this was just a single, special meal that Jesus did the one time.

There are other, deeper textual issues at play here. The Last Supper does not appear in the gospel of John and John shows no knowledge of it or the Eucharist; this means it probably was not an original element of the Passion Narrative Mark adapted but a separate pericope related to Jesus's death that Mark added here.[18]

Next is that the idea of drinking blood, which is taboo in Judaism, would certainly not have played within a purely Jewish context. Paul in the 50s was writing to his mostly Gentile church in Corinth, and by the time

---

18. Alternately, John left it out because it conflicted with his chronology, which is different from the synoptic version, but this still implies that John did not know about the Eucharist as a ritual or sacrament.

the gospels as we have them were redacted the Christian community was beginning to be overtaken by Gentiles rather than Jews. A ritual involving the drinking of blood (even symbolic blood) makes much more sense in that backdrop.

Most importantly, Luke, who was probably a disciple of Paul, *merges Mark's version with elements from Paul's*. For example, Luke alone of the gospel writers has Jesus command his followers to repeat this meal in "remembrance" of him. Luke is also the only one to call the blood in the cup a "new" covenant, like Paul does.

Finally, there are important early sources that show no knowledge whatsoever of the Last Supper or Eucharist. John has already been mentioned, but neither Q nor *Thomas* attest to this. Nor, tellingly, does the *Didache*, which was a manual of early Christian ritual and practice (possibly stemming from the same community as Matthew, which also shows no knowledge of the Eucharist as a ritual). If this ritual was instated by Jesus himself and universal to the Christian community, its absence in the *Didache* is completely inexplicable.

This is all clearly indicative of a branching tradition that has been interpreted differently by different communities (and combined awkwardly by Luke). The Last Supper is known in some places and by some communities, but not in others, and not always connected with any sort of ritual. So where does it come from?

Well, Paul tells us where it comes from in 1 Corinthians 11:23. He says that he "received it from the Lord," meaning from the risen Jesus and not from any other Christians. Since I do not believe Jesus (or anyone else) has ever come back from the dead, I cannot assign this to the historical Jesus.

But we can do better than this. Paul leaves us other clues. He is writing about this ritual in the context of the Corinthians doing it wrong: "*When you come together, it is not really to eat the Lord's supper,*" he tells them in 1 Corinthians 11:20. The problem is not one of performing the rituals wrong, but rather something that should by now make the hairs on our arms stand on end:

> *Now in the following instructions I do not commend you, because when you come together it is not for the better but for the worse. For, to begin with, when you come together as a church, I hear that there are divisions among you.... When you come together, it is not really to eat the Lord's supper. For when the time comes to eat, each of you goes ahead with your own supper, and one goes hungry and another becomes drunk. What! Do you not have homes to eat and drink in?*

> *Or do you show contempt for the church of God and humiliate those who have nothing? (1 Cor 11:17–22)*

The failure of the Corinthians to observe the Eucharist properly is that they are unequal. They are not sharing freely of their food, and they are not eating together. This inequality toward the less fortunate among them shows contempt for the church. They are not practicing commensality.

Recall our exploration of commensality in the mission of Jesus, and it all becomes clear. The Eucharist has evolved from the radical shared meals of the early Kingdom Movement. The first stage probably came from a historical remembrance of the very earliest Christians (the original disciples who knew Jesus) of the types of meals they shared with him, when he broke the bread and poured the wine as the leader of the group.[19] This could even have referred to the last time they did this, shortly before Jesus's death, which took on a special significance after he was executed. These meals remained a part of Christian practice, where they were re-interpreted by Paul and his disciples as a ritual commemorating the death of Jesus and in anticipation of his return. In the time shortly after the destruction of the temple in the year 70, when Mark was writing, it was reinterpreted again as a harbinger of the coming kingdom of God (which was now no longer a present and growing prefigurative movement but a coming apocalypse). This ritual and the story behind it spread, but not everywhere and not always together. This process continued long after the earliest era of Christianity, eventually evolving into its modern form, where people line up and take bread or wafers and terrible wine or grape juice as a sacrament. Gone is commensality, gone is the imperative for all members of the community to be equal, gone again is the original radicality of Jesus.

The Trial(s) of Jesus

> *Pilate asked him, "Are you the king of the Jews?" He answered him, "You say so." Then the chief priests accused him of many things. Pilate asked him again, "Have you no answer? See how many charges they bring against you." But Jesus made no further reply, so that Pilate was amazed. (Mark 15:2–5; Matt 27:11–14; Luke 23:2–4)*

---

19. The Essene Community Rule also prescribes a communal ritual meal which begins with a priest blessing bread and wine.

This one is much easier than the last. It is simply historically untenable. Pilate's portrayal, which intensifies with each successive gospel, is of a just but harangued Roman governor just trying to do his best but pressured into executing Jesus by the bloodthirsty Jews. It reeks of a Gentile and Romanizing church desperate to appeal to Roman polite society that just couldn't get around the historical fact that Pilate had ordered Jesus crucified and so had to create this fiction to absolve him of this crime.

Luke adds a fictitious trial before Antipas as well, and there are also elements of a brief trial before the Jewish authorities in which Jesus's accusers cannot agree on his crimes. This last element is the only one that *may* reflect real history; the confused atmosphere after Jesus's demonstration in the temple could have conceivably created such a situation.

Ultimately it is a moot question. Jesus almost certainly received a cursory trial at best; at worst he was simply arrested and methodically sent to the cross along with whoever else had stirred up any kind of trouble in Jerusalem that day. His followers, afraid of being arrested as well for helping with the temple disturbance, denied being a part of Jesus's entourage and/or fled the scene, and Jesus was summarily executed. The trial is an apologetic fiction meant to blame the Jews and absolve the Romans.

Why?

This chapter must unfortunately end the same way Jesus's life ended: abruptly. I know that this account of the end of Jesus's life is disappointing and perhaps even insulting to many Christians, but I have to be honest about the historical data, which is scarce at best and confused at worst. The Passion Narrative is suffused with mythology, theology, and midrash. Behind it are the brutal facts of Jesus's death: he came to Jerusalem for Passover, miscalculated the cost of performing a prophetic and symbolic destruction of the temple, was betrayed, denied, and abandoned by his followers, and then hung on a cross like a common troublemaker.

Do I really believe it is that simple? Yes, I do. I do not see strong historical evidence that Jesus expected his own death, and as much as I want him to have been too smart to make an error like this that would have led to his death, I am afraid that is merely my wanting Jesus to have been perfect.

But he was not perfect. My minimalist methodology and my materialist convictions preclude me from believing in the supernatural, in gods or miracles or magic or destiny or perfect human beings. Jesus may be the man I look up to more than any others, and he may have even been the most remarkable man ever to have lived, but he was still a human being with faults who made mistakes. His biggest mistake, in my estimation, was what we on the Left might call adventurism: he staged an ill-conceived demonstration in a place that he did not fully understand (Jerusalem was a big city and he was a country bumpkin from Galilee), and his followers proved more cowardly than he expected.

But this cannot be the end of any reconstruction. If Jesus was simply another would-be prophet or revolutionary who started a failed movement and died, he would have joined the ranks of others like Theudas and Judas the Zealot and The Egyptian and few today would know his name. The world today would look radically different, for better or for worse.

But that is not what happened.

Chapter 6

RESURRECTION

Human knowledge is not a straight line, but a curve, which endlessly approximates a series of circles, a spiral. Any fragment, segment, section of this curve can be transformed into an independent, complete, straight line, which then, if one does not see the wood for the trees, leads into the quagmire, into clerical obscurantism, where it is anchored by the class interests of the ruling classes.
—Vladimir Lenin, *On the Question of Dialectics*

STARTING POINT

I have mentioned this already, but I need to elaborate further. This reconstruction of the resurrection of Jesus will begin from the *presumption* that Jesus did not really rise from the dead. I want to be clear by presumption: this is not based on the textual or historical evidence, but the conviction I hold that Jesus was a human being and human beings do not and have not come back from the dead.

I am a Christian. I will say more about what Christianity means to me and why I claim that label, but for now I know that I may have lost any Christians who managed to make it this far without putting this book down in frustration, annoyance, or anger. Coming out as a Christian who does not believe in the bodily resurrection of Jesus has been one of the most interesting experiences I've had; most people, Christians and non-Christians alike, seem unable to even comprehend such a thing. But many Christians have also expressed to me, usually privately, that they agree with me. So please, if you are faithful, put aside your gut instinct to chuck this book in the bin and write me off as a heretic. I want to believe if you've made it this far that you can accept that Christianity means different things to different people. To some of us, it does not rely on the resurrection having actually happened. An attack on the resurrection need not be an attack on Christianity.

I am a Christian, but this is intended to be a secular, scientific, materialist reconstruction of the historical Jesus. In nearly every reconstruction of the historical Jesus I've ever read (and I have read a great many of them), the question of if the resurrection actually happened is left aside for a bare exploration of the textual evidence, or of the effect of the resurrection *experiences* (which I do believe happened) on later Christianity. Any scholar who says that this is the result of there simply not being enough data to make a call is being dishonest; the reality is that they are too afraid to ostracize a Christian audience.

But I am not afraid of that. Nor do I believe that it is possible or honest to reconstruct the historical Jesus without talking about the resurrection, because it has inextricably shaped every aspect of Christianity as we know it. The reason Jesus even needs to be reconstructed in this matter, rather than simply written about like any ancient historical figure, is because nearly all of our information about him is filtered through the lens of people who believed that he had come back from the dead.

So we will examine the evidence. I wish to make explicit that no amount of textual evidence will ever convince me that someone has come back from the dead; I do not expect, nor would I accept, the resurrection of Jesus as a historical event as a conclusion of any of this evidence. When talking about this subject there are three stances to take:

A) Jesus really came back from the dead, and the textual evidence reflects this.

B) Jesus did not come back from the dead, and the stories of him doing so were invented by his followers to serve some purpose.

C) Jesus did not come back from the dead, but his followers had experiences that made them *truly and honestly believe* that he had.

Obviously I reject stance A. I also reject stance B on the basis that there is no actual evidence for it and it does not fit with how ancient people actually thought. The simplest and most likely starting point is that the *resurrection experiences* were real. They do not tell us anything more about the historical Jesus than we already know, but they do help to explain why this is such a complicated task and how Christianity became what it is.

So let's dive in, shall we?

BURIAL

The last chapter, on Jesus's death, began with an exploration of crucifixion. That section could easily have gone here as well, because it bears on the first question of bodily resurrection: burial. As we have seen, the vast, vast majority of crucifixion victims were not buried; it was a part of the special cruelty of crucifixion.

However, our sources do speak of Jesus receiving a burial. Paul mentions it (although he gives no details) in connection with the resurrection, and resurrection presumes burial. The common narrative that everyone knows (wrapping, being laid in a tomb, then the tomb being found empty three days later) comes from only one source, Mark, which is then copied into Matthew and Luke and John. Q and *Thomas* know nothing of it.

Because Jesus's resurrection narrative begins with an empty tomb, our first step is to determine whether or not Jesus was actually buried in a tomb. We cannot examine this apart from the second half of the story, the tomb being found empty, so we take both at the same time.

First we note that it is not impossible that a crucified Jew might receive a burial. Josephus even notes in his autobiography, *Life*, that during the war he begged future emperor Titus to let three of his friends be taken down from the cross as a personal favor. One actually survived. But in this case, the interruption of a proper crucifixion (which includes the destruction of the body by scavenging animals) required the intervention of the future emperor. The thought of someone with no powerful or connected allies receiving similar treatment is highly unlikely.

Fortunately for Jesus, the gospels present him as having just the friend to intervene on his behalf. Here is the narrative, from Mark.

> *When evening had come, and since it was the day of Preparation, that is, the day before the sabbath, Joseph of Arimathea, a respected member of the council, who was also himself waiting expectantly for*

> *the kingdom of God, went boldly to Pilate and asked for the body of Jesus. Then Pilate wondered if he were already dead; and summoning the centurion, he asked him whether he had been dead for some time. When he learned from the centurion that he was dead, he granted the body to Joseph. Then Joseph bought a linen cloth, and taking down the body, wrapped it in the linen cloth, and laid it in a tomb that had been hewn out of the rock. He then rolled a stone against the door of the tomb. Mary Magdalene and Mary the mother of Joses saw where the body was laid.* (Mark 15:42–47; par. Matt 27; Luke 23)

Here are the immediate concerns. First, this story presupposes a trial before Pilate and Pilate's knowledge of who Jesus was, which I have already argued is extremely unlikely. Next, the burial relies on a figure named Joseph of Arimathea, who was apparently both a member of the Kingdom Movement *as well as* a member of the council (the Sanhedrin) that had just orchestrated Jesus's execution. The Sanhedrin was a judicial council composed of seventy-one chief priests and elders, often of the Levite class. In other words, they were the elites, members of the class of people Jesus specifically formed his movement in opposition to. This alone casts a long shadow of doubt on this Joseph of Arimathea. Adding to this, not only are there no other references to this supposed person, but there are not even any other references *anywhere* to a place called Arimathea.

But we will reserve judgment on that for the moment. For now, let us continue to the second half of Mark's story. There is nothing between the last excerpt and this one.

> *When the sabbath was over, Mary Magdalene, and Mary the mother of James, and Salome bought spices, so that they might go and anoint him. And very early on the first day of the week, when the sun had risen, they went to the tomb. They had been saying to one another, "Who will roll away the stone for us from the entrance to the tomb?" When they looked up, they saw that the stone, which was very large, had already been rolled back. As they entered the tomb, they saw a young man, dressed in a white robe, sitting on the right side; and they were alarmed. But he said to them, "Do not be alarmed; you are looking for Jesus of Nazareth, who was crucified. He has been raised; he is not here. Look, there is the place they laid him. But go, tell his disciples and Peter that he is going ahead of you to Galilee; there you will see him, just as he told you." So they went out and fled from the tomb, for terror and amazement had seized them; and they said nothing to anyone, for they were afraid.* (Mark 16:1–8)

First, a note that is of paramount importance. *This is where the gospel of Mark originally ended.* Modern bibles contain an additional twelve verses describing appearances of the risen Jesus to Mary Magdalene and other disciples, but these simply do not exist in the very oldest manuscripts of Mark; they are of a different style than the rest of the gospel; and they may betray knowledge of Matthew and/or Luke (the two unnamed disciples Jesus appears to in the countryside recall Luke's narrative of the appearance on the road to Emmaus). They are later additions.

That's right. The earliest gospel ended with no appearance of the risen Jesus at all, and the ending stated that the only people who saw the empty tomb didn't tell anybody.

But we'll come back to that later. For now, let us see how this pericope is developed through the synoptic tradition. We start by noting that Mark's account is relatively straightforward and shows little sign of redaction; it flows naturally from the earlier part of his narrative and lacks much in the way of apologetics or theological/mythological aspects.

So how does Matthew treat this story? The most noticeable differences are, first of all, that Joseph of Arimathea is no longer a member of the Sanhedrin, but "a rich man" (Matt 27:57). This solves the obvious problem of it making no sense that a member of the Sanhedrin that bullied Pilate into crucifying Jesus would intervene to have him buried, but introduces the new problem that Matthew has placed a rich man in a movement that rich people were not allowed to be in without giving up all of their wealth. Matthew was not concerned with this as he was writing in a context when the church wanted to accept wealthy people, but this cannot go back to the time of Jesus.

Next, Matthew shoehorns in a lengthy narrative of Pilate appointing guards over the tomb of Jesus to make sure that his disciples do not steal his body in order to trick people into thinking Jesus came back from the dead. This makes no sense. Nobody would have been expecting Jesus to come back from the dead, and the historical Jesus did not believe that he was going to come back from the dead. This never happened. Matthew, as he is wont to do, shows his hand shortly after the tomb is found empty, stating that the guards were paid off to lie and say that Jesus's disciples did in fact steal his body, "And this story is still told among the Jews to this day" (Matt 28:15). All this tells us is that by the end of the first century in some places non-Christian Jews were accusing Jesus's followers of having faked his resurrection. Importantly, however, this does not seem to have been widespread, or even early, as we would expect either Mark or Luke (perhaps even Paul) to mention it if that were the case.

Finally, Matthew adds the tiny detail that the tomb in which Jesus was laid was a "new" tomb (Matt 27:60), surely to avoid the embarrassment of having Jesus be lain in an old tomb among other dead people of no importance.

Luke also makes his own "improvements" to Mark's narrative. Joseph is back to being a member of the Sanhedrin, but Luke takes pains to inform us that he did not agree with the rest of them about having Jesus crucified. Luke also, like Matthew, adds the detail that Jesus's tomb is one "where no one had ever been laid" (Luke 23:53), a move surely intended to add gravitas and honor to Jesus's burial.

Matthew and Luke also further develop the second half of this unit, about the empty tomb. Matthew has the angel descend dramatically from Heaven like an earthquake, with a face like lightning. This angel rolls back the stone in front of the women, and his appearance frightens the guards Matthew invented so much that they "became like dead men" (Matt 28:4). He gives the women the instruction to pass on the message, as in Mark, but then Jesus himself also appears, greets the women, and repeats the message. Matthew's intentions are clear: he is trying to solve the narrative problem he created by adding guards to the story, as well as making it impossible that the stone could have been moved in any other way by making the angel do it within the narrative itself.

Luke's additions are different. He has two angels, for some reason, and here the women immediately go to tell "the eleven and to all the rest" (Luke 24:8). This happens not in Galilee, but still in Jerusalem, but they are not believed. This leads to an episode where Peter has to see for himself and runs to the tomb.[1]

This process finally reaches its climax in John, who has developed this pericope much further than the others. I include it in this analysis because we are talking about *process*; the way successive authors add details to a pericope in order to make whatever point they want to make.

In John's account (John 19:38—20:10), Joseph is again no longer a member of the Sanhedrin, but a "secret" disciple of Jesus because of his fear of the Jews. He asks Pilate for permission to bury Jesus, but the tomb is no

---

1. This may be a late addition to the gospel; it is not in all manuscripts and evidences the effort by later Christians to rehabilitate Peter after his denials of Jesus mentioned above.

longer specified as belonging to him. He and another of Jesus's followers, Nicodemus, anoint Jesus before burial, as is proper; here John is solving problems in the original narrative that were embarrassing or unseemly (Jesus being laid to rest without a proper anointing). John also specifies that the tomb is brand new, and now it is no ordinary tomb, but is connected to a garden, recalling the ancient Israelite king Manasseh (2 Kgs 21:18). Jesus is now given a kingly burial.

John also includes an episode similar to Luke's, where Peter and "the disciple whom Jesus loved" go to visit the empty tomb after being told by Mary Magdalene about it.[2] This story is suffused with John's special apologetic about "the disciple whom Jesus loved," a topic that is irrelevant to the current purpose and so I leave aside. The only thing I take from it now is that the story of Jesus's burial clearly undergoes significant development as time goes on.

But in the beginning was the simple version from Mark. Its purpose is clear: to provide an avenue by which Jesus could have been buried. It does not make much sense as a historical account, but it makes perfect utilitarian sense: some narrative device is needed to get Jesus off the cross and into a tomb so that the resurrection can happen and so that Jesus is spared the shame of such a horrific death. Joseph of Arimathea is perfect: he is both a member of the council and so influential, but also a disciple of Jesus. This probably did not raise any eyebrows around the time Mark was written; the Kingdom Movement had become the early church and wealthy or powerful people were no longer excluded; and around four decades had passed and Jerusalem had been destroyed (the Sanhedrin with it), so there was nobody around to protest that there *was no* Joseph of Arimathea on the Sanhedrin at the time. He is a phantom, a fictitious person, created by Mark or the author of Mark's source for the passion, and then incorporated successively into each gospel with additional theological and narrative embellishments. As Barabbas was created to serve a polemical function, Joseph and his tomb were created to serve a narrative function.

How then do we understand Paul's statement that Jesus was buried? Well, burial is presumed in resurrection. Paul believed in the resurrection, and therefore believed that Jesus *must have been buried*. Let us examine deeper.

---

2. This story may have originated in John and knowledge of it influenced whoever later added it to Luke.

In 1 Corinthians 15:3–4, Paul writes: *"For I handed on to you as of first importance what I in turn had received: that Christ died for our sins in accordance with the scriptures, and that he was buried, and that he was raised on the third day in accordance with the scriptures."* In the very first verse of this chapter, Paul explicitly identifies this teaching as the gospel itself.

But what does Paul mean by having "received" this teaching? Well, elsewhere he tells us where he believes the gospel has come from. To the Galatians he writes: *"For I want you to know, brothers and sisters, that the gospel that was proclaimed by me is not of human origin; for I did not receive it from a human source, nor was I taught it, but I received it through a revelation of Jesus Christ"* (Gal 1:11–12).

So it comes to this. We have two sources claiming a burial of Jesus. The first is based on divine revelation and is nonspecific; in my view it is assumed from the belief in resurrection rather than based in any specific knowledge. The second source is a literary creation, again based on the need to explain the resurrection.

Based on this, my judgment is that the burial of Jesus, by Joseph of Arimathea or anyone else, is nonhistorical. The best Jesus could have hoped for was being taken down and thrown into a shallow grave with everyone else who was crucified that day, as Josephus reports sometimes happened. Most likely, however, is that Jesus suffered the same fate as most crucifixion victims. His body was left on the cross as a warning to other would-be prophets, to be, as Josephus put it, "devoured by fowls."

RESURRECTION

I have already said that for Paul and the gospel authors at the very least, resurrection presupposes burial, and I do not believe the burial is historical. What this means is that they started from the point of resurrection and worked backward to explain the burial that they thought *must have happened*. It was not based in any evidence or knowledge of what happened to Jesus's body. They had no idea what happened to Jesus's body. They had resurrection experiences, and surmised from these experiences that Jesus *must have been* buried.

So we end this final chapter with a reconstruction of these resurrection experiences. I have already made it clear that the possibility of Jesus having literally risen from the dead is ruled out from the beginning. But an examination of the textual evidence can help us to make sense of what probably did happen after the death of Jesus, and why it matters.

Again, our earliest source is Paul. The most important text is also from 1 Corinthians 15, and picks up from v. 5, directly after the end of the last quote from that letter we just saw.

> . . . and that he was raised on the third day in accordance with the scriptures, [5] and that he appeared to Cephas [Peter], then to the twelve. Then he appeared to more than five hundred brothers and sisters at one time, most of whom are still alive, though some have died. Then he appeared to James, then to all the apostles. Last of all, as to one untimely born, he appeared also to me. (1 Cor 15:4–8)

Paul is our earliest and only firsthand source for an appearance of the resurrected Jesus. There is some disagreement about whether or not his placement of himself at the end of this sequence of appearances—Peter, the Twelve, five hundred, James, all the apostles, Paul—implies that he understood his experience to have been of the same character as everyone else's. To be honest, I doubt the question would have occurred to Paul or to any other early Christian. It is the type of question someone trying to do a historical reconstruction is interested in, not one a first-century Jewish Christian is interested in. However, because of that I find it unlikely that Paul is intentionally making it seem as though his experience is the same as the others when it really wasn't, a proposition that some have suggested.[3] Paul had personally met Peter and James (Gal 1:18–19) and certainly would have heard about their experiences. I do not think he would have felt the need to embellish his own resurrection experience to make it fall in line with theirs.

Let us consider Paul's experience of the risen Jesus. We have two sources: Paul himself, and the book of Acts (written by Luke). We have already seen Paul's brief recollections of his own experience of the risen Jesus. Paul speaks of the risen Jesus in the passive voice, saying he "was seen" (ὤφθη, *ophthe*) by himself and all of the others. He also says that God "revealed" (*apokalypsis*) Jesus to him in Galatians 1:16.

Acts is more helpful. Luke (the author of Acts) admires Paul greatly and may have been his student or follower. He clearly shows some direct knowledge of Paul's conversion experience, even writing decades later.

---

3. I'm thinking of Dr. William Lane Craig, who said this in a debate with Gerd Ludemmnn in 2002. On the opposite end of the spectrum, John Dominic Crossan, whom I agree with about many things, also takes this position.

RESURRECTION

> *Meanwhile Saul, still breathing threats and murder against the disciples of the Lord . . . was going along and approaching Damascus, [and] suddenly a light from heaven flashed around him. He fell to the ground and heard a voice saying to him, "Saul, Saul, why do you persecute me?" He asked, "Who are you, Lord?" The reply came, "I am Jesus, whom you are persecuting. But get up and enter the city, and you will be told what you are to do." The men who were traveling with him stood speechless because they heard the voice but saw no one. Saul got up from the ground, and though his eyes were open, he could see nothing.* (Acts 9:1–8)

Paul goes into Damascus, blind, and three days later a Christian named Ananias, also instructed by a vision of Jesus, appears and removes Paul's blindness. According to Acts, Paul immediately accepts a baptism, stays in Damascus for several days preaching in the name of Jesus, is almost killed by the (non-Christian) Jews but escapes by being lowered in a basket down a window, and goes to Jerusalem.

Paul's own account is different. He confirms the basket incident in 2 Corinthians 11:32–33, in a speech about all of the trials he's endured as a Christian, but gives no chronological indicators to suggest this happened days after his conversion. Even more puzzling is that Paul places the blame for this incident on the Nabataean (Arab) governor, King Aretas, instead of the Jews. We will obviously trust Paul's firsthand account over Luke's secondhand account, but Paul gives no indication why the Nabataeans would want to arrest or execute him for being a Christian. This account is highly suspect, and here we already have a clear contradiction between Luke's account and Paul's.

Paul does offer a brief description of his own experience of the risen Jesus in 2 Corinthians, shortly after narrating the basket incident. Speaking of himself in the third person to show humility, he says,

> *I know a person in Christ who fourteen years ago was caught up to the third heaven—whether in the body or out of the body I do not know; God knows. And I know that such a person—whether in the body or out of the body I do not know; God knows—was caught up into Paradise and heard things that are not to be told, that no mortal is permitted to repeat.* (2 Cor 12:2–4)

Paul is clearly describing a vision or ecstatic experience, not a sober encounter with a resurrected corpse. Be that as it may, there is also a contradiction here as Paul's experience, which may have been "out of body," could not possibly have been heard by "the men who were traveling with him," as Luke tells it. Luke describes not only blinding light visible only to Paul, but also an auditory component that was audible to anyone who might have been there. This detail is incompatible with Paul's own account that the experience was out of body for all he knew and that the things he heard were for no mortal to repeat.

So we have a detailed account in Luke that is at least somewhat unreliable, describing an auditory apparition and a blinding light that only Paul could see. Paul's own account contradicts at least the auditory aspect of this, lacks any reference to a three-day blindness period, and Paul admits that even he is unsure of the character of his experience. He also implies that previous experiences of the risen Jesus (to Peter, James, and others) were of the same character.

Finally, Paul directly states that Jesus's resurrection was not bodily, at least not the way we would understand it today. His idea of the resurrection is in no way incompatible with the idea of Jesus's body being devoured by the carrion birds, other than the fact that Paul presumes burial. Yet Jesus's earthly body is not what he believes was raised.

> *And as for what you sow, you do not sow the body that is to be, but a bare seed, perhaps of wheat or of some other grain. . . . It is sown in dishonor, it is raised in glory. It is sown in weakness, it is raised in power. It is sown a physical body, it is raised a spiritual body. If there is a physical body, there is also a spiritual body.* (1 Cor 15:37, 43–44)

Paul did not claim to have seen Jesus's physically resurrected body, nor did he claim that any of the other disciples did. Rather, they experienced his *spiritual* body, in the form of light and the sound of his voice.

My conclusion is that the resurrection experiences were ecstatic experiences that convinced the earliest Christians that Jesus was still somehow present in their lives. These could have been dreams, hallucinations, visions sparked by meditation or worship, or simply strong feelings that Jesus's followers had. They interpreted these experiences as revelations from Jesus. Even Paul, who had never met Jesus although was acquainted with him through his experiences persecuting the early Christians, had an experience of this sort.

I do not say any of this to disparage, diminish, or demean these experiences or the religious experiences people still have of figures like Jesus, Mary, or others. In the first century there was no scientific or material understanding of visions or altered states of consciousness. These people did not idealistically dream up wild new thoughts and stupidly believe they came from Jesus or God; nor did they cynically create new teachings for personal or political gain and claim Jesus's authority to legitimate themselves (well . . . okay, *some* of them did do that). They had legitimate experiences that they understood in the way that best made sense to them and their worldview.

I do not believe that these experiences happened within days or even weeks of Jesus's death. I think they took months or even longer, and this is where all of the work we have done reconstructing Jesus and his original ministry has its greatest strength. We will come back to that in a moment, but first, a few final confirmatory notes.

Paul took Jesus's resurrection as a sign of a coming general resurrection. It was never meant to end with Jesus. Jesus was merely the "first fruit" of the coming resurrection (1 Cor 15:20). This was central to Paul's proclamation of the gospel: *"If there is no resurrection of the dead, then Christ has not been raised; and if Christ has not been raised, then our proclamation has been in vain and your faith has been in vain,"* he writes in 1 Corinthians 15:13–14. But it is not merely the fact of Christ's resurrection: it is inextricably tied with the resurrection of all the dead "in Christ" (v. 18). Earlier, in 1 Thessalonians, Paul wrote:

> *For since we believe that Jesus died and rose again, even so, through Jesus, God will bring with him those who have died. For this we declare to you by the word of the Lord, that we who are alive, who are left until the coming of the Lord, will by no means precede those who have died . . . the dead in Christ will rise first.* (1 Thess 4:14–16)

Some of the earliest Christians had died, and there was a question of if they would still be able to enter the kingdom, which has become a future but still imminent event. Here is Paul's answer to that problem: Christ's resurrection has heralded a coming general resurrection, and those Christians who died in anticipation of the kingdom would be the first to enter it. This idea became widespread by the time Mark was written, no doubt intensified by the war against the Romans:

> *Truly I tell you, there are some standing here who will not taste death until they see that the kingdom of God has come with power.* (Mark 9:1)

Yet as time went on this belief in the imminence of the second coming became more and more difficult to maintain. Most or all of the first generation of Christians had died. Many of the latter epistles in the New Testament, such as the Epistle to the Hebrews (not actually written by Paul as some think) and 2 Peter (also not written by Peter) deal with this contradiction. Christianity lost its emphasis on a rapidly-coming kingdom in favor of a kingdom that could come at any time, including "a thousand years" from now or more (2 Pet 3:8). It also progressively lost its revolutionary character and its Jewishness; the wealthy were allowed to join, the torah was de-emphasized, and the focus became about a heavenly afterlife rather than a prefigurative and revolutionary community on earth.

This textual analysis clearly shows at minimum that the earliest Christians, and then Paul, did not experience Jesus's resurrection as the resuscitation of his corpse. I infer that because of their visionary experiences of Jesus, he was slowly elevated from their teacher and the founder of their movement to the Messiah who would return to bring about the kingdom in all its power. The idea that this Messiah could have been left on the cross to be picked at by birds was unthinkable, so the conviction took hold that he *must have been* buried. The idea of Jesus appearing shortly after the crucifixion, walking around and appearing to his disciples, arose decades later, after those first Christians who would have been around at the time in question had died.

Now we will step back for one final general analysis to flesh out and confirm this picture.

WHY JESUS?

Jesus was far from the only person to lead an antiestablishment Jewish revival movement and be executed for it in first-century Palestine. John the Baptist was one. Theudas was one, mentioned in Acts, as well as Josephus. Judas the Galilean was another, as well as his sons. Josephus also speaks of one called "The Egyptian," whose followers were crushed, although he apparently escaped. We know these peoples' names only because of Josephus and/or the early Christian community, and we know very little about them. Josephus implies that there were many more, writing of "ten thousand other disorders in Judea" around this time.[4] Their movements did not survive

---

4. *Antiquities*, XVII.10.

long after the deaths of their founders, not even John's. None of them made a lasting impact on Jewish thought or founded a totally new religion.

Except for Jesus. Many Christians will say that of course this is due to the fact of the resurrection; it inspired such faith that the movement continued and developed into a new religion based on this risen Christ. Christianity grew and flourished where other similar movements failed because Jesus, unlike the others, was raised from the dead, vindicated by God (or even *was* God), and proven correct.

This is where starting from the position of denying the literal truth of the resurrection is crucial. Because we accept that Jesus was a human being and human beings do not and have not come back from the dead, we can look instead to other solutions to this problem. Jesus was not identical to John, Theudas, Judas, or The Egyptian, but like them he created a movement in opposition to the material forces of Palestine and Rome and paid the ultimate price for it. So what set him apart?

Here also, more than anywhere, the common notion of an "apocalyptic Jesus" that preached the imminent end of the world falls apart. It *requires* the resurrection in order to make sense; if Jesus preached the coming advent of the kingdom of God through divine intervention with himself as the viceroy or messiah of this coming event, then his death makes him a failure. I'm okay with Jesus being a failure, but I'm not okay with the idealist supposition that the entirety of Christianity is based on some visions some people had. For that is the only way the alleged apocalyptic Jesus movement can become Christianity—through the resurrection appearances.

I believe that the resurrection *appearances* happened, but why? Why Jesus specifically? That is the question that proponents of the apocalyptic Jesus theory fail to answer in any satisfactory way. If these experiences were unique in some way as to lead to the movement enduring long after the founder's death and eventually forming a brand-new religion (not to mention the largest religion in the entire world), then they are admitting that there was something magically *special* about Jesus or his followers. If they suppose that these experiences were not unique and could have happened to followers of other would-be apocalyptic prophets, then they must (and cannot) explain why this *only* happened in the case of the Jesus movement.

As a materialist, I reject both explanations. I look to the production and reproduction of the essentials of human life. I look to the material conditions and the unique aspect of Jesus's movement itself. Jesus may have been a remarkable person, may even have been the most remarkable man to have ever lived, but he was not magic, or divine. Neither were his followers. And while his teachings and wisdom may have been unique, ideas and wisdom do not create social movements. Practice, refined with theory and manifested as praxis, does.

So this is when I look back on all of this work reconstructing the historical Jesus and see if it makes sense of Jesus's death and resurrection and the movements of the earliest Christians. Here is what I see.

After Jesus's death, his movement continued nearly uninterrupted, because *it was never meant to be about him*. Those disciples that were with him in Jerusalem were probably greatly shaken, but those others, those itinerant ministers traveling the countryside, healing the sick and eating with sinners, they simply kept on doing their work. At some point, even those who had been with Jesus at the time of his death, or at least some of them, got back to work as well, for they still believed in the kingdom of God. It was all around them. People were carrying the mission on. It still worked.

At some point within months or years of Jesus's crucifixion, because they were still engaged in this activity, some of Jesus's followers began having resurrection experiences. These experiences probably varied somewhat, but once it happened to one or two, it began to take on some of the components of mass hysteria and new experiences were influenced by older ones. The tradition differs on whether it was Peter or Mary Magdalene to have the first experience—chronologically the tradition of Peter is earlier but the one of Mary Magdalene has the criterion of embarrassment going for it (a woman's testimony wasn't considered trustworthy in first-century Palestine and so it's unlikely it would have been invented based on nothing). We need not pick one or the other. Perhaps they competed with each other. Perhaps Peter and Mary both had experiences, disagreed about what they meant, and it caused some sort of rift.

Whatever happened there, some of Jesus's closest followers decided to go to Jerusalem and form a commune (Acts 4:32). This included his family and the Twelve. They believed Jesus was telling them something; God had vindicated him and things were changing. It was time to initiate a new phase in the prefigurative kingdom of God. All property was held in common, and missionary and mass work was coordinated from a somewhat centralized location. Yet all of those itinerant prophets were still out there in Galilee, spreading the message semi-independently from the control of Peter and James.

RESURRECTION

And then came Paul. A few years had passed since Jesus's death, and Paul, a devout Pharisee, took issue with some of the things Jesus's followers were saying. They were coming to the belief that the kingdom they had prepared during Jesus's lifetime and after was nearly reaching its climax in some way. Paul, after an initial period of persecuting the nascent Christian church, had his own resurrection experience and converted.

It is hard to say exactly what Paul added to the emergent church and what was there before him, as he is our earliest source. Paul says that it took three years after his conversion before he visited Jerusalem and spoke to Peter and James; he says that his knowledge of the gospel comes from divine revelation and not from any human teacher; and he says that after *fourteen years* he finally explained his version of the gospel, which he'd been preaching that entire time, to James and Peter to get their approval. They seem to have reluctantly approved, but Paul admits that they had to remind him not to forget the poor.

We do not have any direct writings of James or Peter to fall back on; like Jesus, they were peasants from Galilee and probably illiterate. The book of James probably does derive from this early Jerusalem community,[5] but it is removed from them by at least a generation. Still, it displays more continuity with the Kingdom Movement as I have reconstructed it than Paul's ideas about resurrection, the second coming, and the apocalyptic kingdom. James contains a lengthy section about works of the law (including caring for the poor; Jas 2:14–17); healing the sick and forgiving sins (5:14–15); and a brutal excoriation of the wealthy (5:1–6).

I do not wish to contribute to the long-held cliché among some Christians and scholars that Paul represents some seismic rupture with the authentic teachings of Jesus, or that Paul somehow "perverted" the gospel. Paul kept many radical aspects of Jesus's movement intact, mainly its egalitarianism and critique of Roman society. But it is clear that he did interpret the person and message of Jesus on his own, based on his own experiences and beliefs.

Many things are possible. What I find most likely is that the belief in the imminence of the kingdom arose shortly after Jesus's death, before Paul's conversion. It was what prompted the disciples to form the Jerusalem commune. They began to think of Jesus not just as the man who founded their movement, but as the Jewish Messiah who would be returning soon to finish the job that he had started. They were not trying to betray his original

---

5. Penner, *Epistle of James and Eschatology*.

material kingdom; rather the situation changed for them after Jesus's death and they became, like many other Jews, swept up in apocalyptic fervor.

I think Paul developed this even further by formulating educated apologetics about a crucified Messiah, which was an oxymoron in Jewish thought. All this time, the eating-and-healing mission of the original Kingdom Movement continued, but other prophets, not just Paul, were changing it based on their own experiences. The early Christian community was a diverse place, full of non-antagonistic contradictions.

Paul's ideas about Jesus as the crucified Christ come to redeem people of their sins, about him as the exalted Son of God the Father, became too much for the Jews he started off preaching to. But they found an eager audience among Gentiles, and Paul quickly began tailoring his message to them. The inevitable conclusion of this was that Paul began to see no need for the Mosaic Covenant anymore, especially among his Gentile converts. It would be hard to sell them on a movement that required them to undergo circumcision and adopt strict dietary laws. For Paul, what was important was the material equality among believers and faith in this absurd idea of the crucified-and-exalted messiah Jesus.

Meanwhile, as the Kingdom Movement lost its focus on creating dual power structures and became a movement focused on a coming apocalypse, what had originally set it apart from other Jewish millenarian movements vanished. It became like other apocalyptic movements, and the poor rural Jews who had once been its target audience predictably lost interest. After the destruction of the temple in the year 70 CE, the system of dual power which had been set up in opposition to it was made redundant, and this remnant of the original Kingdom Movement finally lost its purpose. The focus of Judaism was turning to torah and study rather than temple and purity.

This is why Christianity became a movement mostly of Gentiles instead of the Jews who had founded it. When it became apocalyptic and based on the character of the risen Jesus Christ, it lost its appeal for the colonized Jews who found it too reminiscent of other failed or failing prophetic messianic movements they saw. They still cared for the sick and shared food, but the context was different. Now it was in expectation of a coming apocalypse instead of a present community they could participate in; now it was done only in expectation and remembrance of a man who had been crucified, but was somehow also the messiah, an idea that flew in the face of centuries of Jewish messianic expectation.

But Gentile audiences who were attracted to foreign religions found it exciting and stirring and became its most dedicated adherents. It spread through the Greek-speaking world and even to Rome, *"where all things hideous and shameful from every part of the world find their center and become popular,"* as Tacitus would later put it. Slowly but surely, Christianity lost its Jewish character.

It also lost the immediacy of its apocalyptic expectation as time went on. Yet the Gentiles that were making up its membership had no special attachment to the idea that the world was about to end; they were the colonizers, not the colonized. Taking Paul's ideas and running with them, Christ became exalted higher and higher until this process reached its natural conclusion with Jesus becoming God himself, taking human form in order to be crucified for the sins of mankind. This idea is violently antithetical to anything Jewish and certainly has nothing to do with the historical Jesus.

The longer this process went on, the further and further Christianity got from the kingdom of God as preached by Jesus. The genius of the Kingdom Movement was in its ability to survive the death of its founder, but this survival came with the near certainty that the successors of Jesus himself would fall into revisionism and the movement would change. Revisionism stems from the removal of class struggle from a revolutionary movement, and this is what happened to Christianity as it became a movement for "everyone." The focus was put on charity and almsgiving instead of dual power, mass work, and prefigurative praxis. The itinerant prophets retired or joined settled church assemblies. The practice of sitting and eating together with the lowest members of society to symbolize fellowship and equality became sacrament rather than praxis. Christianity was born.

This is no one person or faction's fault. Certainly Paul is guilty of some of it, but so were Peter and James and so probably were many other original prophets and leaders whose names are lost to us.

Yet that original idea was never completely lost. Jesus's revolutionary message is still there, buried beneath many layers of text for us to uncover. Christianity may have developed from the idea of a crucified-and-risen messiah into a religion of billions worshiping that cross while hoarding gold, using proselytization as an excuse for colonization, and reproducing the oppressive structures it originally sought to destroy.

But in the beginning there was just Jesus and his followers, ordinary men and women, sitting at a table and sharing meager scraps with the poor, the disabled, the sick, and all of the outcasts of Jewish society.

Epilogue

THE GOOD NEWS

I don't care if I fall as long as someone else picks up my gun and keeps on shooting.

—Che Guevara

TOWARD A NEW CHRISTIANITY

This book is not a biography of Jesus. Nor is it an exhaustive study of every saying and deed attributed to him. Perhaps if there is interest in such a thick book, I will undertake to write it in the future, or expand this one to include everything. For now, however, this will have to do.

What I have done here is offer a materialist reconstruction of the historical Jesus of Nazareth based on the most important and best-attested data. I have paid special attention to the class dynamics within Judaism in order to form my starting point. I began my portrait of Jesus from his actual practice rather than his teachings, for reasons laid out in chapter 4. I started with the best-attested unit of material in the entire tradition, *the Mission*, and saw striking parallels between it and other revolutionary movements throughout history.

Throughout I have adhered to a firmly minimalist methodology. I am a skeptic and a rationalist and a materialist, and although I have no desire to deny wondrous deeds and sayings to the historical Jesus I feel that I am on much safer historical ground if I tread carefully.

I know that the results will not be satisfying to many Christians. I felt the same way when I first dove into the study of the historical Jesus. It felt like this man that I thought I'd known had turned out to be a fake, that there was no basis anymore for a faith built around him or his teachings. I stopped being a Christian and I stopped believing in God.

The reality that affected me most is that in a sense, Jesus was a failure. He created a movement to topple the powers of injustice and oppression in his homeland. This did not happen, and his movement was bastardized into an unjust, oppressive religion that legitimizes the authority of the ruling classes in nearly all of its incarnations. It has caused millions upon millions of deaths in its two thousand–year history, and continues to inflict suffering on hundreds of thousands of people at this very moment. It reinforces structures of colonialism, patriarchy, white supremacy, and capitalism that are eroding so-called "civil society" and destroying the environment humans require to live.

Jesus is no more responsible for this than the original Bolshevik revolutionaries are responsible for the many mistakes made by the Soviet Union throughout its history. They were trying to do something brand new, something that had never been attempted before in the history of the world. They were trying to free themselves and their neighbors from brutal oppression and create a new type of society. So was Jesus.

The proper conclusion of any book about the historical Jesus is a satisfactory answer to the question "So what?" Why does any of this matter? If modern Christianity has little or nothing to do with the historical Jesus, then shouldn't modern Christianity be abandoned? And if Jesus was just a man who tried to create a new type of world and failed, shouldn't he be regarded as any historical failure who fought authority and lost?

My answer to both of these questions is no. I am still a Christian, and I am more comfortable with and passionate about my faith now than I ever was when my beliefs were more orthodox.

Is faith nothing but a set of statements one must believe? Is it merely a doctrine to adhere to in one's own head? Is it the subjugation of reason, intellect, and creativity to a conformist dogma instituted by men of the ruling and colonizing classes throughout history?

If I believed that was the case, then I would probably be one of those grouchy New Atheists who can't resist foisting their poisonous hot takes about religion on anyone who has the misfortune to come into contact with them. Thankfully, I am instead a Marxist and a materialist. So I know that there must be a material basis for faith.

Faith is not belief. Faith is practice. Faith manifests as works. Faith is feeding the hungry, healing the sick, loving the stranger, pleading the case of the orphan and the widow. That is what it meant to the Jewish prophets, and that is what it meant to Jesus.

I concluded that if Jesus preached a faith that had nothing to do with modern Christianity, then perhaps the problem isn't faith, but modern Christianity.

So I no longer believe in God as a theistic being that created the universe. I understand God as a concept arising in class society that embodies different elements of class struggle. To the ruling classes, God is the higher power that legitimizes their authority. To the oppressed classes, God is the promise that they will be liberated. I choose to believe in this God, not as an ontological reality but as an existential concept created by human beings.

Understanding that Jesus preached a radical message of absolute equality scared me at first. I thought he was *too* radical. I disagreed with the parable of the Workers in the Vineyard. It wasn't fair! Those who had worked the longest should get *some* extra compensation, shouldn't they?

This was my liberalism and individualism speaking. I was coming to realize that I didn't like those qualities about myself, so I tried to quell them, and to follow this terrifying revolutionary Jesus as far as he would take me. I started as a milquetoast liberal excited for Hillary Clinton's 2016 presidential campaign. As I searched for answers, for a political movement that most closely correlated with what Jesus tried to do, I became more and more radical. I found Marxism and then Marxism-Leninism and then Marxism-Leninism-Maoism, with its emphasis on serving the masses and building dual power, just like Jesus.

And Jesus is still pulling me along this road. I am convinced that he offers one of the key missing pieces to making revolution in our time.

Marxism has often been opposed to religion and Christianity especially. This often reflects the position of organized Christian denominations in the parts of the world that have had Marxist revolutions. Christianity is often a force for colonialism and the legitimization of the capitalist world order. It also serves to blunt revolutionary passions among the masses. We are all familiar with the famous quote from Marx that religion is "the opiate of the masses." But what happens when we do what we are never supposed to do with Marx and read the quote in its full context?

> Religion is the sigh of the oppressed creature, the heart of a heartless world, and the soul of soulless conditions. It is the opium of the people. The abolition of religion as the illusory happiness of the people is the demand for their real happiness. To call on them to give up their illusions about their condition is to call on them to give up a condition that requires illusions. The criticism of religion is, therefore, in embryo, the criticism of that vale of tears of which religion is the halo.[1]

Do you see it? The part that both antireligious Marxists and anti-Marxist religious people ignore? The abolition of religion *as the illusory happiness of the people* . . .

What if religion could be more than an illusory happiness? Marx, writing in the mid-nineteenth century, may not have been able to conceive of such a religion, but today, in the twenty-first century, with the writings of Albert Schweitzer and Elisabeth Schussler Fiorenza and James Cone and John Dominic Crossan (and many others) as guides, I certainly can. I can see religion being made from the sigh of the oppressed creature into the battle cry of the oppressed creature.

There is a contradiction between the revolutionary essence and the reactionary manifestation of Jesus's teachings. The Christian churches are unquestionably forces of oppression in the world today. Perhaps the most liberal of them can be changed, but not without waging active struggle to reclaim the truly revolutionary roots.

That is the duty of any Christian who wants to get back to the original message of the Kingdom Movement. The church is the temple of our time, and like Jesus, we need to create an alternative system to counteract its corrupted, destructive influence.

We must form new assemblies, just like the original churches founded by Paul and others, centered on egalitarian social practice. In every interaction we should embody the new world we are trying to realize, and create spaces where anyone can escape the cruelty of imperialist-white supremacist-patriarchal capitalism and experience a different way of being.

We must proclaim the destruction of the corrupt powers of this world wherever we go, and take revolutionary action to bring this destruction about. We must empower the oppressed to defend themselves and the

---

1. Marx, *Critique of Hegel's Philosophy of Right*, 1843.

colonized to seize control of their communities. We must feed the hungry and cure the sick, not as charity but as praxis.

We must reclaim our Christian language and symbols, modernizing and adapting when necessary. Jesus is the "Christ" because he was a liberator, not because of any fantasies of original sin. Where the Greek word *adelphos* appears in the Bible, we should recognize that the best translation is sometimes "comrades" rather than "brothers," because Christianity is a revolutionary community. We must stop thinking of God as a white male; we must create God in the image of the oppressed and the oppressed are mostly not men and not white.

We must ruthlessly criticize all that exists, including and especially the entrenched religious structures of modern Christianity. We must challenge their teachings on sex, sexuality, gender, and patriarchy, and welcome all people of all identities as comrades in Christ.

We must recognize that in our day as well as in Jesus's, the primary class contradiction is between colonizer and colonized. Christianity has been a driving force in colonialism, which is the father of modern capitalism. Christianity must be ruthlessly and vigorously decolonized, centering the experience and leadership of colonized people, for they are the image of Christ.

We must bombard the church, ideologically and materially, until it loses its claim to be the only or rightful authority on Christian life. Our aim must be nothing less than a complete and total Reformation of Christianity along revolutionary lines, so far-reaching and total that it makes the Protestant Reformation look like a blip on the radar.

I have met revolutionary Christians from all over the world through my blogging and online communities who are ready to join this movement for a new faith. I dream of a new branch of Christianity, not Catholic or Protestant or Orthodox, dedicated to enacting Jesus's program wherever there is injustice in the world. Perhaps it could be called Proletarian Christianity.

I am convinced such a movement is necessary. As I write this book many of my communities face existential threats from colossal forces of oppression, exploitation, injustice, and domination. The neighborhood I live in is plagued by poverty. My city is rampant with corruption and thousands of people sleep on the streets every night. My country is the worldwide center of reaction and the main exporter of imperialism, colonialism, and white supremacy in the world. I live on stolen land; the indigenous people of this land faced genocide and this historical atrocity has never been accounted for. I live under an inherently unstable economic system that keeps people perpetually impoverished across generations. The mode of production this economic system is based on, capitalism, threatens total ecological destruction, which could lead to billions of deaths in the coming decades as well as war, famine, disease, and genocide.

But when I read the capital-G Gospel, the Good News, against this backdrop, somehow I don't despair. When I study the movement Jesus called the kingdom of God I don't see an archaic apocalyptic movement that failed or the foundations for a genocidal colonizer religion. I see something that can be applied to our struggles today.

So in the end, I don't believe that Jesus was a failure. He did not realize the kingdom that he so beautifully and fully dreamed of in his lifetime. But he left behind a legacy, a link in the long chain of revolutionaries that have fought against the injustices of class society since the first moment some early human began to carry more than he needed.

This is why every Easter I proclaim proudly that Christ is risen, even though I don't believe Jesus came back from the dead. Jesus was executed, but he lives on in every single oppressed person willing to take up his cross and keep carrying it. That is how revolution works. You can kill the revolutionary, but you can never kill the revolution.

Despite all the misery and despair in the world today, when I read the authentic words of the historical Jesus I hear them just as his original listeners heard them. I hear Good News.

Rejoice if you're poor. You have a world to win.

Rejoice if you're hungry. You will be fed.

Rejoice if you're homeless. You will be sheltered.

Rejoice if you're ill. You will be cared for.

Rejoice if you're a migrant. You will be safe to make your home wherever you please.

Rejoice if you are in prison. You will always be a member of our communities.

Rejoice if you're disabled. The world will be remade for you.

Rejoice if you're gay. Your love will be celebrated.

Rejoice if you're colonized. Your people will be free.

Rejoice if you're a sex worker. You will be fully supported, no matter what you do with your body.

Rejoice if you're a woman. You will belong only to yourself.

Rejoice if you're a man. Your masculinity will be affirming, not toxic.
Rejoice if you're non-binary. Your identity will be celebrated.
Rejoice if you're transgender. You know who you are better than anyone else.
Rejoice if you are alone. You will be found.
Rejoice if you are hurting. You will be made well.
Rejoice if you are hopeless. The kingdom of God is at hand.

BIBLIOGRAPHY

Boccaccini, Gabriel. *Beyond the Essene Hypothesis: The Parting of the Ways between Qumran and Enochic Judaism*. Grand Rapids: Eerdmans, 1998.

Bockmuehl, Markus N. A., ed. *The Cambridge Companion to Jesus*. Cambridge: Cambridge University Press, 2003.

Boggs, Carl. "Marxism, Prefigurative Communism, and the Problem of Workers' Control." *Radical America*, special double issue, 11.6 / 12.1 (1977/78) 99–122. https://library.brown.edu/pdfs/1125404123276662.pdf.

Borg, Marcus J. *Jesus: Uncovering the Life, Teachings and Relevance of a Religious Revolutionary*. London: SPCK, 2011.

Brown, Elaine. *A Taste of Power: A Black Woman's Story*. New York: Pantheon, 1992.

Chapman, David W. *Ancient Jewish and Christian Perceptions on Crucifixion*. Wissenschaftliche Untersuchungen zum Neuen Testament 2. Tubingen: Mohr Siebeck, 2008.

Cross, Frank Moore. *The Early History of the Qumran Community*. New Directions in Biblical Archaeology. Garden City: Doubleday, 1971.

Crossan, John Dominic. *The Historical Jesus: The Life of a Mediterranean Jewish Peasant*. New York: HarperCollins, 1991.

———. *How to Read the Bible and Still Be a Christian*. New York: HarperOne, 2015.

DeConick, April D. "The Gospel of Thomas." *Expository Times* 118 (2007) 469–79.

———. "The Original 'Gospel of Thomas.'" *Vigiliae Christianae* 56 (2002) 167–99.

Engels, Friedrich. *The Origin of the Family, Private Property and the State*. Translated by Alick West. 1972. Reprint, Penguin Classics, 2010.

Feeley-Harnik, Gillian. *The Lord's Table: The Meaning of Food in Early Judaism and Christianity*. Washington, DC: Smithsonian Institution Press, 1981.

Flavius Josephus. *Antiquities of the Jews*. Translated by William Whiston for Project Gutenberg. http://www.gutenberg.org/files/2848/2848-h/2848-h.htm.

Fox, Robin. *Kinship and Marriage: An Anthropological Perspective*. Harmondsworth, UK: Penguin, 1968.

Grunewald, Thomas. *Bandits in the Roman Empire*. Abingdon-on-Thames, UK: Routledge, 2004.

Hayes, Christine. *Introduction to the Bible*. Open Yale Courses series. New Haven: Yale University Press, 2012. Kindle edition.

Hengel, Martin. *Crucifixion in the Ancient World and the Folly of the Message of the Cross*. Translated by John Bowden. Philadelphia: Fortress, 1977.

BIBLIOGRAPHY

Kleinman, Arthur, and Lilias H. Sung. "Why Do Indigenous Practitioners Successfully Heal?" *Social Science and Medicine* 13B (1979) 7–26.

Knight, C. "Early Human Kinship Was Matrilineal." In *Early Human Kinship*, edited by N. J. Allen et al., 61–82. Oxford: Blackwell, 2008.

Koester, Helmut. *Introduction to the New Testament*. 2 vols. Hermeneia: Foundations and Facets. Philadelphia: Fortress, 1995.

Lenin, Vladimir. "The Dual Power." In *Lenin Collected Works*, translated by Isaacs Bernard, 24:38–41. Moscow: Progress, 1964. Originally published in the *Pravda* newspaper (Moscow), April 9, 1917. https://www.marxists.org/archive/lenin/works/1917/apr/09.htm.

Luck, Georg. *Arcana Mundi: Magic and the Occult in the Greek and Roman Worlds*. 2nd ed. Baltimore: Johns Hopkins University Press, 2006.

Mack, Burton L. *The Lost Gospel: The Book of Q and Christian Origins*. New York: HarperCollins, 1993. Kindle edition.

Mao, Zedong. *Collected Works of Mao Tse-Tung (1917–1949)*. Washington, DC: Joint Publications Research Service, 1978.

———. *Selected Works of Mao Tse-Tung*. Beijing: Foreign Languages, 1965.

Marx, Karl. *Critique of Hegel's Philosophy of Right*. Translated by Joseph O'Malley. Oxford: Oxford University Press, 1970.

———. *The German Ideology*. With Friedrich Engels. New York: Prometheus, 1998. Originally written in 1846.

Opie, Kit, and Camilla Power. "Grandmothering and Female Coalitions: A Basis for Matrilineal Priority?" In *Early Human Kinshi*, edited by N. J. Allen et al., 168–86. Oxford: Blackwell, 2008.

Patterson, Stephen J. *The Gospel of Thomas and Christian Origins: Essays on the Fifth Gospel*. Nag Hammadi and Manichaean Studies 84. Leiden: Brill, 2013.

Penner, Todd C. *The Epistle of James and Eschatology*. Journal for the Study of the New Testament Supplement Series 121. Sheffield: Sheffield Academic, 1996.

Smith, W. Robertson. *Lectures on the Religions of the Semites*. London, 1894.

Sukenik, Naama, and Orit Shamir. "Qumran Textiles and the Garments of Qumran's Inhabitants." *Dead Sea Discoveries* 18 (2011) 206–25.

Tomson, Peter J. "The Didache, Matthew, and Barnabas as Sources for Early Second Century Jewish and Christian History." In *Jews and Christians in the First and Second Centuries: How to Write Their History*, edited by Peter J. Tomson and Joshua Schwartz, 348–382. Compendia Rerum Iudaicarum ad Novum Testamentum 13. Leiden: Brill, 2014.

Van de Sandt, Huub. *Matthew and the Didache: Two Documents from the Same Jewish-Christian Milieu?* Minneapolis: Fortress, 2005.

———. *Matthew, James, and Didache: Three Related Documents in Their Jewish and Christian Setting*. With Jurgen K. Zangenberg. Society of Biblical Literature Symposium Series 45. Atlanta: SBL, 2008.

Vermes, Geza. *The Authentic Gospel of Jesus*. London: Penguin, 2004.

———. *Jesus the Jew: A Historian's Reading of the Gospels*. Glasgow: Collins, 1973.

Wacholder, Ben Zion. "Ezekiel and Ezekielianism as Progenitors of Essenianism." In *The Dead Sea Scrolls: Forty Years of Research*, edited by D. Dimant and U. Rappaport, 186–96. STDJ 10. Leiden: Brill, 1992.

Wink, Walter. *Engaging the Powers: Discernment and Resistance in a World of Domination*. Minneapolis: Augsburg Fortress, 1992.

SUBJECT INDEX

Aslan, Reza 8, 32
Augustus Caesar, 35, 38–41

Babylonian Exile, 30, 34, 60
Beatitudes, 102
birth of Jesus, 44–48
Black Panther Party, 113
Bolshevik Revolution, 93, 167
Borg, Marcus, 26, 48, 64
Brown, Elaine, 113

Canaanites, 32
capitalism, 28–29
Carrier, Richard, 18
C.H. Dodd, 56, 59, 64
class society, 23
commensality, 73–74
Communist Party of China, 112
criterion of dissimilarity, 7
criterion of embarrassment, 7, 51, 76, 105, 132, 142, 162
Crossan, John Dominic, xi, 31, 48, 56–57, 64, 67, 156
Crucifixion, 133–36, 150

Dead Sea Scrolls, 8, 85–86, 122, 145
Didache, 12, 58, 69, 71–72
dual power, 90–91

Ehrman, Bart, 18, 47
Engels, Friedrich 8–9, 127–28
eschatology, 55–64
Essenes, 82–90, 117
Eucharist, 142–45
exorcism, 74–75

family, 125–31
Farrer hypothesis, 12
forgiving sins, 78–81

Gospel of Thomas, 12
Hasmoneans, 35, 47
Hayes, Christine, 49
healing, 74–78
Herod Antipas, 37, 52, 105
Herod the Great, 35–36, 47, 81
historical materialism, 8, 10, 25, 73–74

James the Just, 12, 15, 17, 46, 72, 125
Jesus mythicism, 14–18
Jesus Seminar, 7, 13, 102
John, gospel of, 11–12
John the Baptist, 51–54, 56–57, 62–64
Josephus, 1 13, 15–20, 25, 53, 150
Joseph of Arimathea, 151–54
Judas Iscariot, 141–42
Julius Caesar, 35, 38–39
Justin Martyr, 133

King David, 32–33
kingdom of God, 54–57, 62–64
Koester, Helmut, 56, 64

Last/Lord's Supper, 67
Lenin, Vladimir, 90
Lord's Prayer, 58
lumpenproletariat, 106, 113

Mao, Zedong, 10, 112–13, 120, 123
Messianic expectation, 37
modes of production, 22–23, 28

SUBJECT INDEX

Nag Hammadi Library, 8

O'Neill, Tim, 18
Origen, 17, 59

pacifism, 114, 117–18
Passover, 115, 138–39
Paul, authentic letters, 12
Paul, biographical details about Jesus, 15
pericopes, 13, 48, 50
Pharisees, 65, 82, 94
Philo, 84
Pontius Pilate, 37, 115, 117, 136–37, 146
prefigurative politics, 88
private property, 23
proletarian, 8–9

Q Gospel, 11
Quest for the Historical Jesus, 7

realized eschatology, 56
Reumann, John, 55

Revisionism, 165

Sadducees, 82
Sanhedrin, 151–54
Schweitzer, Albert 7
Sepphoris, 105
Septuagint, 46
Sermon on the Mount, 49, 115, 118–23
sin and sinners, 79–80, 89, 106
socialism, 29
Sodom, 27
Son of Man, 56, 59–61
synoptic gospels, 11, 44, 50

Tacitus, 13, 20
tekton, 9, 94, 105
Testimonium Flavianum, 16, 19
Twelve Apostles, 111

Vermes, Geza 61, 64

Zapatistas, 91
Zealots, 41–42, 82, 114–15, 133

ANCIENT DOCUMENT INDEX

HEBREW BIBLE

Genesis
2:10–14	31
3:17–18	31

Exodus
21:24	121

Leviticus
19:2	120
19:9	26
24:20	121
25:18	26
25:35	26

Deuteronomy
15:1	26
21:22–23	135
23:19	26
25:5	129

1 Samuel
8:11–18	28

1 Kings
21:3	29

Psalms
37:28	108

Ecclesiastes
10:12	108

Isaiah
2:2–4	42
7:14	46
11:1–9	42–43

Jeremiah
7:11	140–141
7:14	141

Ezekiel
16:49–50	27

Daniel
7:7	59
7:13–14	59
7:24–25	60

Amos
2:6–7	28
8:4–7	27

Micah
2:1–2	27

Zechariah
9:9	137

ANCIENT DOCUMENT INDEX

NEW TESTAMENT

Matthew

3:14	51
5:11–12	102
5:18	119
5:22–25	120
5:39	121
5:43	108
5:48	123
7:14–19	95
9:1	159
10:5–10	68
10:34	116
10:34–36	126
11:12	117
11:19	64
15:11	63
18:12–14	110
18:15–20	124
20:1–6	109
23:12	112
26:52	115
26:56	115
28:4	153
28:15	152

Mark

1:4	51
1:7	51
1:9	51
1:15	55
2:15–17	64
2:17	110
2:18–20	65
3:1–2	108
3:33–35	125
4:21–25	107
4:26–29	98
4:30–32	97
6:3	105
6:16	62
6:40–44	66
9:35	111
9:43	123
10:15	106
10:21–25	103–4
10:42–44	111
11:1–8	137
11:15–17	140
14:22	67
14:22–25	143
14:29–30	142
15:2–5	145
15:6	115
15:7	115
15:42–47	150–51
16:1–8	151

Luke

6:21	102
6:24–25	103
6:43–45	95
7:34	63
10:7–8	63, 68
10:1–9	68
11:20	75
13:21	98
14:21b	91
14:26	125
16:16	117
16:17	119
19:41–44	138
22:27	111
23:53	153
24:8	153

Acts

4:32–35	104
9:1–8	157
18:25–26	53

1 Corinthians

9:6	71
9:11	71
9:14	71
11:17–22	144–45
11:20	144
11:23–26	143
15:3–4	155
15:4–8	156
15:13–14	159
15:37	158
15:43–44	158

2 Corinthians
12:2–4	157

Galatians
3:28	130
1:11–12	155

1 Thessalonians
4:14–16	159

2 Peter
3:8	160

DEAD SEA SCROLLS
4QMMT
55, 56, 57	89

GRECO-ROMAN WRITINGS
Josephus
Antiquities of the Jews
14.2	139
15.11	81
17.9	138–39
17.10	160
18.5	52–53, 78
18.6	36
18:63–64	16
20:9:1	17

Jewish War
2.8	83–84

Tacitus
Annals
15:44	20, 165

Florus
Epitome
34	40

Pliny the Elder
Natural History
5.15	84–85

EARLY CHRISTIAN WRITINGS
Gospel of Thomas
9	96
14	63
16	116
22a	106
22b	130
41	107
54	102
57	99–100
63	99
64	100–101
71	140
107	109

Didache
11	71
12	71

www.ingramcontent.com/pod-product-compliance
Lightning Source LLC
Chambersburg PA
CBHW062045220426
43662CB00010B/1665